Mathematics for Retail Buying

Mathematics for Retail Buying

Third Edition

Bette K. Tepper
Associate Professor
Fashion Buying and Merchandising
Fashion Institute of Technology

Newton E. Godnick
Professor
Fashion Buying and Merchandising
Fashion Institute of Technology

Fairchild Publications
New York

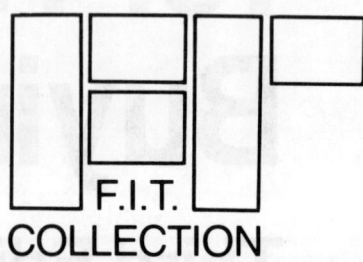

First Edition
Copyright © 1973 by Fairchild Publications
Division of Capital Cities Media, Inc.

Second Printing 1975

Third Printing 1977

Second Edition
Copyright © 1979 by Fairchild Publications
Division of Capital Cities Media, Inc.

Second Printing 1980

Third Printing 1982

Fourth Printing 1983

Fifth Printing 1985

Third Edition
Copyright © 1987 by Fairchild Publications
Division of Capital Cities Media, Inc.

All rights reserved. No part of this book may be reproduced in any form without permission in writing from the publisher, except by a reviewer who wishes to quote passages in connection with a review written for inclusion in a magazine or newspaper.

Library of Congress Catalog Card Number: 86-83026

Standard Book Number: 87005-572-0

Printed in the United States of America

CONTENTS

Unit One: Merchandising for a Profit 1

  I. Basic Profit Factors and Their Meaning 1
     A. Components of Each Basic Profit Factor 3
        1. Operating Income 3
           a. Gross Sales 3
           b. Customer Returns and Allowances 3
           c. Net Sales 4
        2. Total Cost of Merchandise Sold 9
           a. Billed Cost 9
           b. Inward Freight and Transportation Charges 9
           c. Alteration and Workroom Costs 9
           d. Cash Discounts 9
        3. Operating Expenses 14
           a. Direct or Controllable Expenses 14
           b. Indirect Expenses 14
     B. Basic Profit Factors and Their Relationship 14
  II. Profit and Loss Statements 16
     A. Skeletal Profit and Loss Statements 16
     B. The Skeletal Profit and Loss Statement Expressed in Percentages 17
     C. Final Profit and Loss Statement 24
     D. The Importance and Calculation of Gross Margin 26
  III. How To Increase Profits 33

Unit Two: The Retail Method of Inventory 49

  I. What Is the Retail Method of Inventory? 50
  II. General Procedure in Implementing the Retail Method of Inventory 52
     A. Finding an Opening Inventory Figure 52
     B. Maintaining a Perpetual Book Inventory Figure 52
     C. Forms Used in the Retail Method of Inventory 52
        1. Journal or Purchase Record 53
        2. Transfer of Goods 54
        3. Price Change Forms 55
        4. Charge-Back to Vendors 57
        5. Daily Sales Reports 58
        6. Employee Discounts 58
     D. Calculating a Book Inventory Figure 59
  III. Shortages and Overages 65
     A. Causes of Shortages and Overages 66
        1. Clerical Errors 66
        2. Physical Merchandise Losses 66
     B. Calculating Shortages and Overages 66
  IV. An Evaluation of the Retail Method of Inventory 73
     A. Advantages 73
     B. Limitations 73

Unit Three: Retail Pricing and Repricing of Merchandise 78

  I. Retail Pricing 78
     A. The Structuring of Price Lines 78

B. Setting Individual Retail Prices and/or Price Lines 79
C. Advantages of Price-Lining 80
D. Basic Pricing Factors and Their Relationship.. 80
   1. Calculating Retail When Cost and Dollar Markup Are Known 80
   2. Calculating Dollar Markup When Retail and Cost Are Known 81
   3. Calculating Cost When Retail and Dollar Markup Are Known 81
II. Markup 82
   A. Basic Markup Equations.. 82
      1. Calculating Markup % on Retail Using the Retail Method of Inventory 82
      2. Calculating Markup % on Cost 82
   B. Markup Calculations Used in Buying Decisions 82
      1. Calculating Markup % When Individual Cost and Individual
         Retail Are Known 83
      2. Calculating Markup % on a Group of Items with Varying Cost
         and/or Retail Prices 84
      3. Calculating Retail When Cost and Desired Markup % Are Known 86
      4. Calculating Cost When Retail and Markup % Are Known.............................. 86
      5. Calculating Deviations from Aggregate Individual Markups
         (Averaging Markups).. 94
         a. Averaging Costs When Retail and MU% Are Known 94
         b. Averaging Retail(s) When Costs and MU% Are Known 98
         c. Averaging Markup Percents When Retail and MU% Are Known.............. 102
   C. Types of Markup 106
      1. Cumulative Markup 106
      2. Initial Markup 108
      3. Maintained Markup 110
III. Repricing of Merchandise... 113
   A. Markdowns 113
      1. The Purpose of Markdowns 113
      2. Causes of Markdowns 113
      3. Timing of Markdowns 114
      4. The Amount of the Markdown 114
      5. Markdown Calculations 115
         a. Calculating the Dollar Markdown 115
         b. Calculating Markdown Percentage 115
         c. Calculating Markdown Cancellation 116
         d. Calculating Net Markdown 117
   B. Employee Discounts... 122
   C. Additional Markup... 122
   D. Markup Cancellation.. 122
   E. Price Change Procedures 122
      1. Authorizing Price Change 123
      2. Recording of Price Change 123
      3. Changing of Prices on Tickets 123
      4. Distributing Copies 123
   F. The Relationship of Repricing to Profit 123

Unit Four: Invoice Mathematics—Terms of Sale... 141

I. Terms of Sale 141
   A. Different Types of Discount... 141
      1. Quantity Discount 141
      2. Trade Discount 142
      3. Cash Discount.. 144
         a. Calculating Net Cost When Billed Cost and Cash Discount Are Known..... 144
         b. Calculating Net Cost When List Price Is Quoted and Cash
            Discount Is Given 144
         c. Calculating Net Cost Considering Quantity and Cash Discounts................ 145

      B. Net Terms... 146
  II. Dating 150
     A. Different Types of Dating... 151
        1. C.O.D. Dating... 151
        2. Regular (or Ordinary) Dating.. 151
        3. Extra Dating.. 152
        4. E.O.M. Dating 152
        5. R.O.G. Dating 153
        6. Advanced or Post Dating 153
     B. Net Payment Dates.. 154
 III. Anticipation 160
 IV. Shipping Terms 166

Unit Five: Dollar Planning and Control 171

   I. Six-Month Seasonal Dollar Plan... 171
     A. The Procedure, by Element, of Dollar Planning 175
        1. Planning Sales 175
        2. Planning Stocks 176
           Determining the Turnover Figure 177
             a. Calculating Turnover When Average Stock and Sales for the
                Period Are Known.. 178
             b. Calculating Average Stock When Planned Sales and Turnover
                Are Known 178
             c. Calculating Average Stock When Monthly Inventories Are Known 178
           Methods of Stock Planning 180
           1. Setting Individual First of Month Stock Figures by Stock-Sales
             Ratio Method 180
             a. Calculating Stock-Sales Ratio When Retail Stock and Sales
                for a Given Period Are Known 182
             b. Calculating B.O.M. Stock When Planned Sales and Stock-Sales
                Ratio Are Known 182
           2. Setting Stock Figures by Weeks Supply Method 182
             a. Calculating the Number of Weeks Supply................................. 183
             b. Finding Planned Stock, Given Turnover and Weekly Rate of Sales 183
        3. Planning Markdowns 189
        4. Planning Markup on Purchases 190
        5. Planned Purchases.. 191
           a. Calculating Planned Monthly Purchases (Retail) 191
           b. Converting Retail Planned Purchases at Cost 192
           c. Adjusting the Planned Purchases 192
  II. Open-to-Buy Control 197
     A. Calculating Open-to-Buy at the Beginning of the Month 198
     B. Calculating Open-to-Buy During the Month.. 198
        1. OTB for Balance of Month Based on Predetermined Planned Purchases 198
        2. OTB for Balance of Month Based on Planned Closing Stock 198

Unit Six: Periodic Merchandising and Operating Information 217

   I. Reports Used for Merchandise Control.. 218
     A. Dollar Sales by Classification 218
     B. Classification-Price Line Report 218
     C. Classification-Stock Status Report.. 218
     D. Monthly Sales and Stock Report... 218
     E. Fashion Report.. 218
  II. Reports Used for Dollar Control... 225

- A. Total Department Merchandise Statistics Report 225
- B. Individual Store Merchandise Statistics Report 225
- C. Operating Statement 229
- D. Profit and Loss Statement 232

Appendix: The Use of Basic Arithmetic in Merchandising 235

- I. Fractions 235
  - A. Adding Fractions 237
  - B. Subtracting Fractions 237
  - C. Multiplying Fractions 241
  - D. Fractional Quantities 241
  - E. Dividing Fractions 242
- II. Decimals (Decimal Fractions) 245
  - A. Changing a Common Fraction to Decimal Form 245
  - B. Changing a Decimal to a Fraction 245
  - C. Adding Decimals 246
  - D. Subtracting Decimals 246
  - E. Multiplying Decimals 246
  - F. Dividing Decimals 247
- III. Percentages 251
  - A. Changing a Decimal to a Percent 251
  - B. Changing a Percent to a Fraction 251
  - C. Changing a Percent to a Decimal 251
  - D. Basic Elements of Percent Problems 252
    1. Finding the Percentage 252
    2. Finding the Base 252
    3. Finding the Rate 253

Appendix: How to Use a Mini-Calculator 262

- I. Procedure for Simple Arithmetic Calculation of Whole Numbers 262
  - A. Addition Process 262
  - B. Subtraction Process 262
  - C. Multiplication Process 263
  - D. Division Process 263
- II. Procedure for Simple Arithmetic Calculation of Whole Numbers and Fractional Parts 263
- III. Procedure for Simple Arithmetic Calculation of Percentages 263
  - A. Multiplication Process 263
  - B. Division Process 264
  - C. Subtraction of a % from a Whole Number 264

Glossary 265

Reference Readings 269

PREFACE

In the first edition of *Mathematics for Retail Buying*, we stated that operating figures are the language of the retail merchandiser, regardless of the size of the store. In running a business today, in a highly competitive business environment, it is more important than ever to have a basic knowledge of the mathematical factors involved in profitable merchandising. Without this background, it is difficult to comprehend the operations of either a small store or a department in a large store. This fundamental mathematical background gives insight into *how* merchandising problems are solved mathematically and *why* merchandising decisions are based on figures. The most skilled and experienced merchandiser knows that the mastery of mathematical techniques and figure analysis is a worthwhile tool. Persons in related careers who acquire mathematical perception as it pertains to profit factors will better deal with merchandising situations.

Mathematics for Retail Buying delineates the essential concepts, practices and procedures as well as the calculations and interpretations of figures related to the many factors that produce profit. It is written from the viewpoint of the merchandiser who buys goods for resale, namely, the buyer. The choice of material and the depth of each subject are deliberately confined to that which has practical value for the performance of occupations in or associated with retail merchandising. The book was primarily developed as a learning device to meet the needs of career-oriented students who will be directly, or indirectly, involved in the activities of merchandising at the retail level. It can serve as a guide in training junior executives, and can be a constant source of reference for a young assistant buyer or the small merchant who operates an independent store.

The contents are realistic because they have been based on:

- the personal experience of both authors, who were buyers in major retail organizations;
- the opinions of retail executives as to the information necessary to prepare prospective retail merchandisers;
- the insights manufacturers have gained which helped to better service and communicate more effectively with their retail accounts;
- the tested use of the material by the authors and other faculty members teaching at the Fashion Institute of Technology, by faculties at other schools, and by retail executives and training departments;
- the favorable comments about the value of the material to performance in various careers by the alumni of the Fashion Buying and Merchandising curriculum at the Fashion Institute of Technology.

Mathematics for Retail Buying should enable the student to:

- recognize *which* basic and elementary factors of the buying and selling process affect profit;
- understand the *relationship* of the profit factors and improve profit performance by the manipulation of these factors;
- become familiar with the use and function of typical merchandising forms encountered in stores;
- become aware of the practices and procedures in stores;
- become familiar with applications of data processing in retailing;
- know and apply the basic mathematical concepts used in solving merchandising problems;
- acquire the terminology used to communicate in merchandising mathematics.

Every effort has been made to build the contents of the book into a foundation of easy understanding, not merely into formulas. Without sacrificing completeness, the material has been structured into a simplified outline form. The step-by-step presentation uses: brief explanations stated in basic terms; precise definitions; typical merchandising forms illustrating procedures and techniques; and concepts applied to examples to express the mathematical principles. An outstanding feature of the book is that it has the combined advantages of a *handbook* and the benefits of a *workbook*. Within each unit, after a major topic, there is a series of problems that test the understanding of the fundamental principles discussed in that portion. At the end of each unit, there is a large collection of review problems which utilizes practical merchandising situations and common problems and which helps to reinforce learning of the entire unit. Below each problem, throughout the book, workspace is provided for calculations. When these pages are torn out, they permit the text material to remain intact. A glossary of the important terms is appended.

In revising this book, particular attention has been paid to the comments of the various users, including our own personal teaching experiences. The important changes in this edition are:

- the problems have been reworked and many of the older ones have been eliminated;
- the numbers used throughout the text, and in the problems are updated and reflect current industry data;
- a new section entitled, *How to use a Mini-Calculator* has been added to the *Appendix* in order to facilitate usage of this important tool;
- the revised explanation for the gross margin calculation has been amplified to focus on its current significance in industry today;
- bonus and discussion problems have been added to each unit;
- the explanation of the *Retail Method of Inventory* is more detailed;
- the variations in calculating markup percent for groups of items reflect practical industry situations used to merchandise effectively;
- the discussion on and calculations of the various types of markups that pertain to an overall departmental operation have been developed in sequence;
- additional information and figures that pertain to the structure and analysis of seasonal merchandise plans have been included.

As all authors should be, we have been sensitive to, interested in and even fascinated by (and sometimes amused with) comments from colleagues and students at the Fashion Institute of Technology and from many other colleges concerning the sequencing of study units in our book. The old puzzlement about "the chicken or the egg" has surfaced time and time again. Why the *Profit* Unit first? Why not the *Retail Method* Unit? or *Dollar Planning?* or *Pricing?*

We pondered this matter rather endlessly before we attempted the first revision a few years ago. What is probably the obvious dawned on us and, we think, led us to a very basic principle about the buying/merchandising process . . . that it has no *one* beginning point and no *one* finishing point. It is, of course, a circular phenomenon, an unending, deeply interrelated continuum within which all factors influence all other factors.

In practice, few will disagree that the merchandising cycle really must begin with the formulation of a *dollar* merchandising plan. Although the budgeting for this plan initially covers a six-month selling period, it is merely part of an ongoing process of monitoring, analysis and evaluation directed to the purpose of meeting the merchandiser's objective of achieving a pre-determined gross margin which should, in turn, generate an appropriate net profit, as long as other factors remain within expectable ranges.

We mention this here, perhaps somewhat gratuitously, in order to point out to instructors and students alike (and to merchants who use our book for in-service training purposes) that the study of retail mathematics may be begun at any point on the "circle." A simple extension of this concept must lead to a further awareness that a merchant's job, too, is a fascinating continuum in which *every* facet can be influenced by the merchant on his/her road toward achieving pre-determined merchandising objectives. Not many industries can provide their executives on all levels with as high a degree of control of their own business destinies.

The material is divided into six units. Each unit covers a particular, basic mathematical factor that affects the profits of a retail store. The relationships among these profit factors are stressed throughout the book. The units of study and their subject matter are:

- *Unit One, Merchandising for a Profit*—logically begins the study by introducing the concept of profit, and deals with the calculation, interpretation and analysis of the profit and loss statement.
- *Unit Two, The Retail Method of Inventory*—explains the procedure, mechanics and systems of determining the total value of the stock on hand and of shortages calculated through the retail method of inventory.
- *Unit Three, Retail Pricing and Repricing of Merchandise*—discusses the importance of markup to profitable merchandising and the calculations used to achieve the desired results when setting initial retail prices or repricing goods.
- *Unit Four, Invoice Mathematics—Terms of Sale*—concerns itself with the discounts, dating and shipping terms that a retail buyer must know when buying at wholesale.
- *Unit Five, Dollar Planning and Control*—includes the analysis of possible sales, the planning and control of stocks and purchases, and the techniques used to accomplish these objectives.
- *Unit Six, Periodic Merchandising and Operating Information*—gives illustrations of merchandising information used in merchandise and dollar control and an interpretation of figures in a merchandising operation.

Also, we retained the *Appendix, The Use of Basic Arithmetic in Merchandising*, designed to provide supplementary material which reviews the elementary processes used in the business arithmetic of merchandising. We have added a new section, *How to Use a Mini-Calculator* which facilitates the usage of this important tool.

The idea for this book originated with the many faculty members who helped develop some of this material to meet a need when teaching merchandising mathematics at the Fashion Institute of Technology. The authors are indebted to those faculty members for their contributions and to the many students and alumni for their constructive criticism and suggestions which were used in preparing this book. Our thanks also go to the store executives who gave advice and support. Special thanks to the many faculty members, students and industry people whose enthusiastic response provided the incentive to complete this revision; a final acknowledgment to our editor, Joseph Miranda, for his diligence and professionalism.

Bette K. Tepper
Newton E. Godnick

Mathematics for Retail Buying

UNIT ONE

Merchandising for a Profit

Why is the study of the calculation of profit necessary?

The student eventually will have many opportunities to become involved with the concept of profit. *As an employee* of a private organization, you should be aware of corporate profits. For example, you may be a member of a profit-sharing plan, a form of incentive common today in many industries. *As an individual,* you may be a possible investor of personal funds in publicly-owned corporations. To you, *as an employee of a publicly-owned corporation,* profit is a most significant goal in the sale of shares. Since the beginning of the 20th Century, the government requires *any type of entrepreneur* to declare the results of his business ventures. These results are taxed. Good form in accounting requires a statement of net profit before taxes and after taxes.

As a merchandiser in retailing, one of your major responsibilities is to attain a profit for the department* you supervise. As a potential merchandising executive, you will use the calculation of profits in the following ways:

- It will permit, by exchange of data, comparison between stores to determine strengths and weaknesses.
- It indicates the direction of the business and whether it is prosperous or bankrupt.
- It provides a statement for analysis so any changes in management or policy can be made.
- It may result, after analysis, in the improvement of profit.

In this unit we shall acquire knowledge about the basic profit elements, their relationship to each other in skeletal as well as final profit and loss statements, and their manipulation to produce improved profits. When we complete the study of these topics, understand their meanings, learn the calculations, and see the interrelationships that exist, we will be able to determine, through analysis, whether an organization is operating at a profit or loss.

I. BASIC PROFIT FACTORS AND THEIR MEANING

The three basic merchandising factors that directly affect profit results are: *operating income* (retail stores refer to this as *sales volume,* which is a net sales figure), *cost of merchandise sold,* and *operating expenses.*

The function of the retail store is to sell goods to consumers at a profit. These consumer purchases are the store's source of operating income, known as the store's SALES VOLUME. This is a net sales figure.

The RETAIL is the price at which stores offer merchandise for sale to the consumer. GROSS SALES are the total of all the retail prices charged consumers on individual items of merchandise multiplied by the number of units actually sold, or the entire dollar amount received for merchandise sold during a given period. Since stores usually give customers the privilege of returning merchandise, when the merchandise is returned to stock and the customer gets his money back or is given a credit, these returns of sales are called CUSTOMER RETURNS. In addition, if *after* a sale has been made, the customer is then given a reduction in price, this is known as a CUSTOMER ALLOWANCE. NET SALES is the sales total for a given period after both customer returns and allowances have been

---

*Department—Merchandise Department: A grouping of related merchandise for which separate records are kept pertaining to expense and merchandising data, for the purpose of determining the profit of this grouping. It is not a mere physical segregation.

deducted from gross sales. When retailers compute profit, the net sales figure is the *more* significant, since a firm can only realize a profit on the goods which remain sold at the retail prices charged.

Merchandisers must determine the retail price for the items purchased, and they must also be concerned with how much they can afford to *pay* a vendor for merchandise. This is referred to as the COST. COST OF GOODS SOLD is the invoice cost of purchases with necessary adjustments.

The retailer must maintain a place of business from which the goods are sold, and in order to maintain this store, he must incur OPERATING EXPENSES. Operating expenses fall into two major categories and are charged to a merchandise department to determine the net profit for an individual department.

Expenses that come into being with the department and cease if it is discontinued are called DIRECT or CONTROLLABLE EXPENSES. Some of these are: salaries of the buyer, assistant buyer and salespeople; departmental advertising, selling supplies, deliveries to customers, etc. Store expenses that exist and continue to exist, whether a new department is added or an old one is discontinued, are INDIRECT EXPENSES. These store expenses are pro-rated to all selling departments on the basis of their sales volume. Some of these are: store maintenance, insurance, and salaries of top management.

A. Components of Each Basic Profit Factor

It is necessary to dissect each of the basic factors that affect profit because each one consists of elements that contribute to profit.

1. Operating Income

a. Gross Sales—The total initial dollars received for merchandise sold during a given period.

CONCEPT: Gross Sales = Total of all the prices charged consumers on individual items × Number of units actually sold

PROBLEM: On Monday, a department sold 30 scarves priced at $4 each, 25 scarves priced at $7 each, and 5 scarves priced at $10 each. What were the gross sales for that day?

SOLUTION:
30 pcs. @ $4 each = $120
25 pcs. @ $7 each = 175
5 pcs. @ $10 each = 50
GROSS SALES = $345

b. Customer Returns and Allowances—Since the customer in either of these transactions gets either a complete refund of her purchase, or a partial rebate, a deduction must be made from sales since there has been some cancellation of sales. This dollar figure is expressed as a *percent of gross sales*.

CONCEPT: Customer Returns and Allowances = Total of all refunds or credits to the customer on individual items of merchandise × Number of units actually returned

PROBLEM: On Saturday, the coat department refunded $98 for one coat, $75 each for two coats, and $55 each for two coats. The other returns for the week amounted to $400; and the weekly total of allowances given was $57. What was the dollar amount of customer returns and allowances?

SOLUTION:

$98 × 1 = $ 98
75 × 2 = 150
55 × 2 = 110

	Customer returns for Saturday	= $358
(plus)	Total weekly customer returns	= 400
(plus)	Total weekly customer allowances	= 57
	CUSTOMER RETURNS & ALLOWANCES (for week)	= $815

CONCEPT: Customer Returns and Allowances Percent = The dollar sum of customer returns and allowances expressed as a *percent of gross sales*

$$\text{Cust. Ret. \& Allowances \%} = \frac{\$\text{Cust. ret. \& allow.}}{\text{Gross sales}}$$

PROBLEM: Last week the glove department had gross sales of $40,750. The customer returns and allowances for the week totaled $1,630. What was the combined percent of allowances and merchandise returns for the week?

SOLUTION: $$\frac{\$\text{Cust. returns \& allowances}}{\text{Gross sales}} = \frac{\$1,630}{\$40,750}$$

CUSTOMER RETURNS &
ALLOWANCES % = 4%

c. **Net Sales**—The sales total for a given period *after* customer returns and allowances have been deducted from gross sales.

CONCEPT: Net Sales = Gross sales − Customer returns and allowances

PROBLEM: A neckwear department sells $65,000 worth of merchandise. Customer returns amounted to $6,500. What were the net sales of this department?

SOLUTION:
Gross sales	= $65,000
(minus) Cust. returns & allowances	= − 6,500
NET SALES	= $58,500

In retailing, the operating income is known as NET SALES. The net sales figure, also called SALES VOLUME, is used to designate the size of a particular store or a merchandise department. For example, Dept. #37, for last year, had a sales volume of $1,000,000. This dollar figure is generally the sales volume for the *year*.

Since net sales are determined by the adjustment of customer returns and allowances to gross sales, it is also possible through this relationship to calculate, if desired, a gross sales amount when the *dollar* net sales and the % of customer returns and allowances are known.

CONCEPT:

$$\text{Gross Sales} = \frac{\text{Net sales}}{100\% \text{ (gross sales)} - \text{Cust. returns \& allowances \%}}$$

PROBLEM: The net sales of Dept. #93 were $460,000. The customer returns and allowances were 8%. What were the gross sales of this department?

SOLUTION: $$\frac{\text{Net sales}}{100\% - \text{Customer returns \& allowances \%}} = \frac{\$460,000}{100\% - 8\%}$$

$$\text{Gross Sales} = \frac{\$460,000}{92\%}$$

Gross Sales = $500,000

PRACTICE PROBLEMS

1. Customer returns and allowances for Department #620 amounted to $4,500. Gross sales in the department were $90,000. What percentage of goods sold was returned?

2. The gross sales for Store B were $876,500. The customer returns and allowances were 10%.

    a. What was the dollar amount of returns and allowances?
    b. What were the net sales?

3. The net sales of Department X were $46,780. The customer returns amounted to $2,342. What were the gross sales?

4. The gross sales of Store C were $2,500,000. The customer returns and allowances amounted to $11,360. What were the net sales?

5. The net sales of Department Y were $36,000. The customer returns and allowances were 10%. What were the gross sales?

6. Discussion Problem: Explain why a merchant should have cause for alarm if customer returns become excessive. How does a merchant determine what constitutes an excessive return percentage? What can be done by the department itself to correct a problem rate of returns?

7. Bonus Question—The customer returns for the Fall season were 10% on gross sales of $900,000. For the Spring period gross sales were $850,000 and the customer returns were $70,000. What were the customer return percentages for the entire year?

2. **Total Cost of Merchandise**—In actual practice, cost of merchandise is affected by the following factors:

   a. **Billed Cost**—The price at which goods are purchased and which appears on the invoice (vendor's bill) for merchandise.

   PLUS

   b. **Inward Freight or Transportation Charges**—The amount that a vendor may charge for delivery of merchandise. Inward freight plus billed cost is called the *billed delivered cost*.

   PLUS

   c. **Alteration and Workroom Costs**—The amount that selling departments may be charged for work which is necessary to put the merchandise in condition for sale. (Assembling, polishing, making cuffs, etc.) It is accepted practice to treat this figure as an addition to cost since it applies only to goods that have been sold and *not* to all purchases.

   MINUS

   d. **Cash Discounts**—Discounts which vendors may grant for payment of an invoice within a specified time. For example, 2% deducted from the total of the billed cost, providing payment was made in the time agreed. The discounts are offered in the form of a *percent of the billed cost only,* but the dollar discount earned is used in the calculation of the total cost of sales. For example, a 2% cash discount on a billed cost of $1,000 is translated into a $20 deduction.

	Billed cost	$1,000
×	Cash disc. %	× .02
=	Dollar Discount	$20.00

CONCEPT: Total Cost of Merchandise = Billed cost + Inward transportation charges + Workroom costs − Cash discounts

PROBLEM: A blouse department, for a six-month period, had billed costs of merchandise amounting to $80,000; transportation charges of $2,000; earned cash discounts of 7½%, and had $500 in workroom costs. Find the total cost of merchandise.

SOLUTION:

	Billed costs	= $80,000
(plus)	Inward freight	= + 2,000
	BILLED DELIVERED COST	= $82,000
(plus)	Workroom costs	+ 500
	GROSS MERCHANDISE COSTS	= $82,500
(minus)	Cash discounts (7½% × $80,000)	− 6,000
	TOTAL COST OF MERCHANDISE =	$76,500

NOTES

PRACTICE PROBLEMS

1. A luggage buyer purchased 72 attaché cases costing $40 each. Cash discount earned was 2%. Freight charges (paid by the store) were $95. Find the total cost of goods on this order.

2. A buyer of women's blouses placed the following order:
   36 blouses costing $10.75 each
   48 blouses costing $15.50 each
   24 blouses costing $17.50 each
   Shipping charges, paid by the store, were 6% of billed cost.
   Find:

   a. Dollar amount of shipping charges.
   b. Delivered cost of the total order.

3. A gift shop had workroom costs amounting to $575. The billed cost of merchandise sold amounted to $59,000, with cash discounts earned of $1,180, and freight charges of $650. Find the total cost of the merchandise.

4. A small dress shop made purchases amounting to $3,700 at cost, the cash discounts earned were 8%, the workroom costs were $100, and there were no transportation charges. Determine the total cost of the merchandise.

5. A buyer of sporting goods placed the following order:
   18 canvas backpacks costing $22 each.
   12 pup tents costing $34 each.
    6 camp stoves costing $55 each.
   Shipping costs, paid by the store, were $60. Cash discount taken was 1%. Find:

   a. Billed cost on the total order
   b. Total delivered cost of the merchandise

6. Discussion Problem: Explain why control of inward transportation costs and workroom (alterations) costs is vital. Can a merchandiser help to control these factors? How?

7. Why is cash discount calculated on billed cost?

3. **Operating Expenses**—Expenses incurred by the retailer for maintaining a place of business, paying salespeople, etc. Operating expenses fall into two major categories and are charged to a merchandise department in order to determine its net profit. They are expressed as a *percent of net sales*. These two major categories are:

   a. **Direct or Controllable Expenses**—Expenses that come into being with the department and cease if it is discontinued. These might include: selling and buyer's salaries, advertising, selling supplies, delivery to customers, and rental of space for the department.

   b. **Indirect Expenses**—Store expenses that will continue to exist even if the particular department is discontinued. These might include: store maintenance, insurance, depreciation of equipment, salaries of senior executives, etc.

   CONCEPT: Operating Expenses = Direct expenses + Indirect expenses

   PROBLEM: A children's department has net sales of $300,000 and indirect expenses that are 10% of net sales. Direct expenses are as follows: selling salaries = $24,000; advertising expenses = $6,000; buying salaries = $12,000; other direct expenses = $18,000. Find the total operating expenses of the department in dollars and as a percentage.

   SOLUTION:
Indirect expenses (10% × $300,000)	$30,000
Direct expenses: Selling	24,000
Advertising	6,000
Buying	12,000
Other	18,000
TOTAL OPERATING EXPENSES	= $90,000

   $$\frac{\text{Operating expenses}}{\text{Net sales}} = \frac{\$90,000}{\$300,000} = 30\%$$

B. **Basic Profit Factors and Their Relationship**
   The following example shows the relationship of the three fundamental factors upon which the amount of profit depends. In order to make comparisons these factors are expressed as percents as well as in dollars. We realize that the *net sales* figure is the *basis for determining profit computation,* and so is considered 100%. The other factors involved are shown and stated as a percent of net sales.

   EXAMPLE:
Net sales volume (Operating income) =	$10,000	100%
(minus) Cost of merch. sold =	− 5,500	− 55%
(minus) Operating expenses =	− 4,300	− 43%
PROFIT =	$ 200	2%

NOTES

II. PROFIT AND LOSS STATEMENTS

Business firms must keep an accurate record of their sales income, costs of merchandise, and operating expenses, in order to know how much profit is being earned. Periodically, the income and expenses are summarized on a form known *in retailing* as a Statement of Profit and Loss. This statement is frequently called an income statement in other types of organizations. It summarizes the transactions of a business during a given period of time, in terms of making money or losing money. The accounting department of the business firm will keep a continuous record of the sales income and the expenses, and at given intervals compiles a statement which shows whether these transactions have resulted in a profit or in a loss. The period it covers might be a year, three months, or one month. A Profit and Loss Statement is not to be confused with a Balance Sheet which shows the assets, liabilities and net worth of a business.

We will analyze the Profit and Loss Statement *not* as a bookkeeping procedure, but in terms of how the data it contains can be used by the merchant to improve his merchandising operation. It is a fundamental merchandising concept that one of the buyer's chief responsibilities is to see to it that a department earns a profit. It must be remembered that profit is earned only on the merchandise that is *sold* during the accounting period under consideration.

Essentially, a Profit and Loss Statement shows the difference between income and expense(s). If income exceeds expenses, the result is a profit. If expenses exceed income, the result is a loss. The five major component parts of a Profit and Loss Statement are: net sales, cost of merchandise sold, gross margin (the difference between net sales and cost), operating expenses, and the resultant profit or loss figure. The difference between net sales and the total cost of merchandise sold is GROSS MARGIN. This figure must be large enough to cover the operating expenses incurred by the seller and to allow for a reasonable profit. It is calculated for a given period by subtracting the total cost of the merchandise sold from the net sales for the period. Gross margin is also frequently called GROSS PROFIT because it is an indicator of the final results.

CONCEPT: Gross Margin = Net sales − Total cost of merchandise sold

PROBLEM: A department had net sales of $300,000 and the cost of merchandise sold is $180,000. Find the dollar gross margin.

SOLUTION:
Net sales	=	$300,000
(minus) Cost of merchandise sold	= −	180,000
GROSS MARGIN	=	$120,000

A. Skeletal Profit and Loss Statements

A skeletal profit and loss statement does not "spell out" in detail all of the transactions, but it is a quick method of determining where a department stands at any particular time with regard to profit and loss. It merely contains the five major component parts. It is expressed in both dollars and percents.

EXAMPLE:
Net sales	=	$10,000	100%
(minus) Cost of merchandise sold	= −	6,000	− 60%
GROSS MARGIN	=	$ 4,000	40%
(minus) Operating expenses	= −	3,500	− 35%
NET PROFIT	=	$ 500	5%

B. The Skeletal Profit and Loss Statement Expressed in Percentages

The real value of a profit and loss statement is that it can be used as a comparison with previous statements or against industry-wide figures to help improve profit, or any of the other factors mentioned in the example. It, therefore, becomes vital to think in terms of percentages in addition to the dollar amounts. For example, if a buyer were to say that he had a net profit of $2,869 for a given business period, his statement would have no real meaning unless he were to state the dollar amount for every one of the other contributing factors. His profit figure could be phenomenally high or dismally low by industry standards, depending on the dollar net sales volume of his department. We would not be able to discern where his departmental operations had excelled or faltered unless we had the other factors involved available to us. The only meaningful way to compare his departmental performance, therefore, is to compare the respective results expressed as a percentage of the net sales volume. This way, we can pinpoint the fact that profit can vary upward or downward as one or more of the three major factors vary, that is, net sales, cost of merchandise sold, or operating expenses.

CONCEPTS:

$$\text{Cost of Merchandise Sold \%} = \frac{\text{Cost of merchandise sold (in dollars)}}{\text{Net sales}}$$

$$\text{Gross Margin \%} = \frac{\text{Gross margin (in dollars)}}{\text{Net sales}}$$

$$\text{Operating Expense \%} = \frac{\text{Direct \& indirect expenses (in dollars)}}{\text{Net sales}}$$

$$\text{Net Profit \%} = \frac{\text{Net profit (in dollars)}}{\text{Net sales}}$$

PROBLEM: The Glove Department in Store "A" had net sales of $160,000; cost of goods sold was $88,000; operating expenses were $64,000. The Glove Department in Store "B", for the same business period, had net sales of $260,000; cost of goods sold was $135,200; operating expenses were $109,200. Which store produced a higher net profit percentage?

SOLUTION:

	STORE A		STORE B	
Net sales =	$160,000	100%	$260,000	100%
(minus) Cost of goods sold = −	88,000	55% −	135,200	52%
Gross margin =	$ 72,000	45%	$124,800	48%
(minus) Oper. expenses −	64,000	40% −	109,200	42%
NET PROFIT =	$ 8,000	5%	$ 15,600	6%

As a basis of comparison, percentage figures give the clearest picture. Upon examination of the above skeletal profit and loss statement, the reader can see that the Glove Department in Store "A" spent 55 cents of every dollar of sales on the cost of merchandise sold, and in Store "B" spent 52 cents. Respectively, they spent 40 cents and 42 cents of every dollar of sales on operating expenses. Gross margin and net profit become more easily comparable as does each individual transaction recorded in a more complete profit and loss statement. We see that net sales always is the base figure, that is, all other figures in the skeletal profit and loss statement are expressed as a part (percent) of net sales.

PRACTICE PROBLEMS

1. Note the following figures:

   Net profit   2.5%
   Gross margin $7,000
   Operating expenses $6,600

   Find:

   a. Cost of goods in dollars
   b. Percentage of operating expenses

2. The net profit in a department for the Spring/Summer period was $20,000. This represented 2% of net sales. Operating expenses totaled $480,000.
   Find:

   a. Dollar amount of gross margin
   b. Net sales

3. The linen department in a store had net sales of $80,000. There was a 2% loss and the gross margin was 46.5%. What were the operating expenses of the department in dollars and as a percentage?

4. Calculate the percentage of operating expenses in a store with the following figures:

Gross sales	$476,000
Customer returns	4,000
Advertising costs	10,000
Salaries	101,000
Miscellaneous expenses	6,160
Utilities	9,000
Insurance	11,000
Rental	70,000

5. Set up a skeletal statement showing both dollars and percentages.

Net profit	$5,500	
Net profit		2.5%
Operating expenses		47.5%

6. Suppose that the estimated net sales for a coming year are $100,000; estimated cost of merchandise purchases is $52,000; the total estimated operating expenses are $43,000 and the buyer wants a net profit of 5%. Determine the percentage of gross margin on sales he needs to achieve this desired profit.

7. Set up a skeletal profit and loss statement showing each factor in dollars and percentages.

   Net sales $85,000
   Net profit   1,700
   Cost of goods sold 45,000

8. What was the profit or loss in dollars of a department if gross sales were $218,000; customer returns and allowances were $3,000; cost of goods sold amounted to 55% and the operating expenses amounted to 41%?

9. Find the percent of cost of gross margin when:

Gross sales	$435,000
Customer returns and allowances	49,000
Billed cost of goods	195,000
Freight charges	1,800
Cash discounts	4%

10. Discussion Problem: In measuring gross margin performance, which is more significant: the dollar amount or the percentage figure? Why?

NOTES

C. Final Profit and Loss Statement

A final profit and loss statement follows. The figures show the basic factors which have been amplified so that every transaction is clearly seen. In preparing a final profit and loss statement, it is necessary that the many factors be in a *standard arrangement* so that it is possible to have an easily *analyzed* picture of the *results*.

The opening and closing figures of stock on hand* are included when calculating final profit because the firm only realizes a profit on merchandise which is *sold* during a particular accounting period. This is the only way that one is able to use this statement as a comparison with other stores, and it is the only way one can detect weaknesses which need strengthening, and strengths which bear repetition.

For a better understanding of the detailed Profit and Loss Statement shown below, refer to the accompanying explanation of terms.

FIGURE 1. PROFIT AND LOSS STATEMENT

	Cost	Retail	Cumulative M U %	Explanation
Income from Sales			48%	
Gross Sales			$450,000	Total initial sales
(minus) Cust. Ret. & Allowances			− 25,000	Mdse. returned by customer to retailer
Net Sales			$425,000 (100%)	Dollar value of sales that "stay sold"
Cost of Merchandise Sold				
Opening Inventory	$52,000	$100,000		Mdse. in stock at beginning of period counted at retail from which a cost figure is calculated
New Purchases $258,000				Cost of mdse. purchased
(+) Inward Transportation 2,000				Cost of transporting goods to premises
$260,000				Cost of purchases & their amount of inward transportation
Total Cost of Mdse.	$260,000	$500,000		
Total Mdse. Handled	$312,000	$600,000		Opening inventory + total cost of purchases
(minus) Closing Inventory	− 65,000			Mdse. in stock at end of of operating period
Gross Cost of Mdse. Sold	$247,000			Value of mdse. handled minus closing inventory
(minus) Cash Discount	− 13,000			Discounts rec'd. from paying bills in specified time
	$234,000			
(+) Alteration & Workroom Costs	+ 1,000			Cost of preparing mdse. for sale
Net Cost of Mdse. Sold	$235,000		−235,000 (55.3%)	Gross cost of mdse. sold minus cash discounts plus cost of preparing goods for sale
Gross Margin			$190,000 (44.7%)	Difference between sales and total cost of mdse. sold (often called Gross Profit)
Operating Expenses				
Total Direct Expenses	$101,250			All outlays necessary to sell and deliver mdse. to customers
Total Indirect Expenses	67,500			
Total Operating Expenses			$168,750 (39.7%)	
Net Profit			$ 21,250 (5%)	Net Profit = The remaining dollar amount after total expenses and cost of mdse. sold are deducted from net sales.

---

*Final profit calculations use a *Total Merchandise Handled* amount to determine the net cost of merchandise sold.

NOTES

D. The Importance and Calculation of Gross Margin

Gross Margin is the major focus of the merchandiser. Simplistically, from his viewpoint, the gross margin is the net sales minus the cost of goods sold. Gross margin results are planned in advance by management in order to allow for a reasonable profit. Therefore, any factor that can influence its outcome is carefully controlled.

In the calculation of gross margin, one must recognize that the goods sold during a given period could be merchandise in stock before the *beginning* of that period and/or new purchases during this time. The opening and closing inventory figures are crucial in the determination of the gross margin figure. *(The Retail Method of Inventory will be further explained in Unit II.)*

To calculate the gross margin on the combination of merchandise in stock at the start of and purchases during the period under consideration, the steps would be as follows:

STEP 1: Begin with a retail opening inventory figure—e.g. $100,000

STEP 2: Determine a *cost* opening inventory figure—e.g.
$100,000 × (100% − MU %)
= $100,000 × 52%
= $ 52,000

STEP 3: Add to the opening inventory figures (cost & retail) all new purchases at *cost* and *retail*—e.g. new purchases—$260,000 cost, $500,000 retail—to find Total Merchandise Handled (TMH) at Cost and Retail.

STEP 4: Subtract the sum ($475,000) total of net sales ($425,000), markdowns ($45,000) and shortages ($5,000) from the retail figure of total merchandise handled ($600,000) to find the *retail* closing inventory ($125,000) figure.

STEP 5: Determine a *cost* closing inventory figure, e.g.
$125,000 × (100% = MU %)
= $125,000 × 52%
= $ 65,000

STEP 6: Subtract the closing inventory ($65,000) at cost from TMH ($312,000) at cost to find cost of merchandise sold ($247,000).

*STEP 7: Find the margin ($178,000) by subtracting the cost of merchandise sold ($247,000) from the net sales ($425,000).

STEP 8: Add the cash discounts ($13,000) to the merchandise margin $178,000 which is $191,000.

STEP 9: Subtract the workroom cost ($1,000) to find the gross margin of $190,000 (See *Retail Method of Inventory, Unit II, page 39*).

From an accounting viewpoint, when calculating gross margin, the cash discounts and workroom costs are adjusted *after* the margin on the merchandise itself is determined. Nonetheless, since merchants frequently negotiate cash discounts or influence the workroom factor, their impact on the gross margin must be considered.

---

*In the calculation of a maintained markup, the margin on sales is determined *before* making adjustments for cash discounts earned and alteration costs.

CALCULATING GROSS MARGIN ON STOCK PLUS PURCHASES

	Cost	Retail	
Opening Inventory	$52,000 $\begin{bmatrix} \$100,000 \times (100\% - MU\%) \\ \$100,000 \times 52\% \end{bmatrix}$	$100,000	
(Plus) New Purchases and Freight	+260,000	+500,000	
Total Mdse. Handled	312,000	600,000	
Minus:			
Net Sales		425,000	100.00%
Markdowns		45,000	10.58%
Shortages		5,000	1.17%
		−$475,000	
(Minus) Closing Inventory	65,000 $\begin{bmatrix} \$125,000 \times (100\% - MU\%) \\ \$125,000 \times 52\% \end{bmatrix}$	125,000	
Gross Cost of Merchandise Sold	$247,000		
Margin (Net Sales minus Gross Cost of Merchandise Sold)		$178,000	41.9%
(Plus) Cash Discounts		+ 13,000	
		$191,000	
(Minus) Workroom Cost		− 1,000	
Gross Margin		$190,000	44.7%

PRACTICE PROBLEMS

1. Find the net profit or loss as a percent, and the gross margin as a dollar amount:

Gross sales	$200,000
Customer returns & allowances	15,000
Opening inventory (at cost)	38,000
Billed cost of goods	99,000
Inward transportation	5,000
Cash discount	6,000
Closing inventory (at cost)	36,000
Payroll	48,000
Occupancy	28,000
Wrapping and packing	1,200
Utilities	2,000
Delivery	2,800

2. Construct a *Profit and Loss Statement* using the following departmental figures and showing the Net Sales, Total Cost of Goods Sold, Gross Margin, Expenses and Profit:

Gross sales	$ 82,000
Customer returns & allowances	4,000
Inward freight	2,000
Workroom costs	1,000
Opening inventory (at cost)	17,000
Closing inventory (at cost)	14,000
Purchases (at cost)	36,000
Cash discounts	8%
Advertising	5,000
Rent	12,000
Salaries	17,000
Miscellaneous expenses	2,500

3. Construct a final profit and loss statement from the figures listed below and calculate the major factors as percentages as well as in dollar amounts.

Opening inventory	$ 74,200
Gross sales	248,000
Advertising	15,000
Misc. expenses	18,000
Purchases (at cost)	120,000
Closing inventory	78,000
Customer returns	25,800
Salaries	26,000
Transportation charges	8,000
Rent	39,000
Cash discounts	3%

4. Find the Gross Margin in dollars and percents for Store #5 from the following records:

Opening inventory:	$ 156,000 at cost
	300,000 at retail
New purchases:	780,000 at cost
	1,500,000 at retail
Net sales	1,275,000
Markdowns	135,000
Shortages	15,000
Cash discounts	39,000
Alteration & workroom costs	3,000
Cumulative MU %	48%

NOTES

III. HOW TO INCREASE PROFITS

It is practically impossible to list everything a retailer needs to know to merchandise at a profit because the nature of retailing is such that each new day brings a fresh challenge. Since the factors that govern profits are variable, net profits do not represent any fixed sum. Nevertheless, after reviewing a profit and loss statement, and being able to see how these factors affect profit, certain measures can be taken to improve profits. Basically, there is always an interrelationship between the three factors: sales, cost of merchandise sold, and operating expenses. The adjustments made must consider all three factors in relationship to each other. Fundamentally, the approach to improved profits can be:
- increasing *sales* while there is only a proportionate increase in the cost of the merchandise, and little or no increase in expenses;
- decreasing the *cost of merchandise sold* without decreasing sales (e.g., to sell a larger proportion of higher markup merchandise, or to decrease the net cost of goods sold by lowered shipping charges and/or greater cash discounts);
- lowering or reducing *expenses.*

As a frame of reference, listed below is various groups of major retail stores and their profit performance.

	Profits			Profit to Sales	
	Last Year	This Year	% Chg.	Last Year	This Year
Department stores.........	$1,580,722	$1,470,655	+ 7.5	3.3%	3.5%
Mass merchandisers	2,033,300	1,896,700	+ 7.1	2.8	2.8
Specialty stores	568,774	555,579	+ 2.4	4.4	5.0
Discount stores..............	432,774	335,336	+29.1	3.4	3.3
Off-price stores	32,073	24,143	+32.9	5.4	5.2
Miscellaneous................	461,537	478,326	− 3.5	2.3	2.6
Total	5,109,000	4,762,739	+ 7.3	3.0	3.2

NOTES

PRACTICE PROBLEMS FOR REVIEW OF UNIT ONE

1. The following figures are for your department:

Net sales	$490,000
Billed cost of goods	265,000
Freight charges	11,160
Rent	56,640
Salaries	111,600
Miscellaneous expenses	25,260
Cash discounts	37,000
Insurance	27,800
Advertising	16,740
Opening inventory (cost)	117,000
Closing inventory (cost)	120,000

   a. Calculate the total cost of merchandise sold.
   b. Find the operating expenses in dollars.
   c. Determine the profit or loss in dollars and as a percentage.

2. If profit is $8,000 and profit percentage is 4%, what is the net sales figure?

3. If expenses are $85,340 and the gross margin is $90,960, what is the operating profit or loss?

4. Find the net profit or loss in dollars and as a percentage when:

Opening inventory (cost)	$ 70,000
Operating expense	180,000
Closing inventory	72,000
Net sales	400,000
Inward freight	5,000
Purchases, at cost	210,000

5. Gross sales are $25,619; customer returns and allowances are $2,791.32; purchases at billed cost are $12,585; freight inward is $932.45; cash discounts earned average 2%. What is the gross margin in dollars?

6. If a department experiences a loss of 3% for a six month period and its gross margin is 43%, what must be its expense percentage?

7. Gross margin in the shoe department was $185,000. Operating expenses amounted to $178,000 and the net profit was 2% of net sales. What were the net sales?

8. Determine the net sales when:

Operating expenses	$57,750
Gross margin	$56,650
Net loss	1%

9. Find the gross margin as a percentage when:

Gross sales	$283,000
Customer returns	7,000
Billed cost of goods	137,000
Inward freight	5,000
Workroom charges	3,000
Cash discounts	6%

10. Set up a final profit and loss statement using the following figures, giving both dollar amounts and percentages for:

   a. Net profit or loss
   b. Cost of goods sold
   c. Gross margin
   d. Operating expenses

Inward freight	$ 3,000
Workroom and alteration charges	600
Opening inventory (at cost)	14,400
Closing inventory (at cost)	14,600
Customer returns	8,000
Gross sales	82,000
Purchases (at cost)	35,000
Promotional expense	3,500
Rent and utilities	10,000
Payroll	15,500
Miscellaneous expenses	2,000
Cash discounts	3%

   Analyze the figures in Problem 10. Discuss the relationship of expenses to net profit; discuss the size of the gross margin. Suggest ways to improve profit.

11. Determine the dollar profit or loss in a department whose sales were $1,950,000; cost of merchandise sold was 50%, and operating expenses were $925,000.

12. Prepare a skeletal profit and loss statement showing both dollars and percentages for a department showing the following figures.

Net sales	$280,000
Cost of merchandise sold	150,000
Loss	3%

13. The handbag department shows the following figures:

Gross margin	$11,500
Operating expenses	11,000
Net profit	2%

    Find the net sales.

14. A boutique shows these figures:

Gross sales	$104,000
Customer returns	5,000
Billed costs	49,000
Inward freight	10,000
Advertising	7,500
Rent	12,000
Alterations	1,000
Salaries	16,000
Misc. expenses	5,000

    Prepare a profit and loss statement. Did this store operate at a profit?

15. Determine the net sales:

Operating expenses	$82,000
Gross margin	80,500
Net loss	1%

16. Find the gross margin percentage:

Gross sales	$566,000
Customer returns	10%
Billed cost of goods	258,000
Inward freight	9,000
Workroom charges	2,200
Cash discounts	6%

17. Set up a profit and loss statement, showing dollar amounts only, using the following figures:

Gross sales	$127,000
Closing inventory (at cost)	29,000
Opening inventory (at cost)	33,000
Miscellaneous expenses	5,000
Customer returns	6,000
Purchases (at cost)	60,000
Rent and utilities	23,000
Payroll	30,000
Transportation charges	1,700
Cash discounts	8%
Advertising	6,000

18. Construct a skeletal profit and loss statement from the figures below, expressing all factors in both dollars and percentages.

Billed cost of goods	$ 90,000
Workshop charges	2,400
Cash discounts	1,800
Freight charges	3,000
Direct expenses	36,000
Customer returns	9,000
Indirect expenses	31,200
Gross sales	177,000

19. Find the gross margin in dollars and as a percentage.

    Net profit $24,000
    Net profit   1.5%
    Operating expenses   47.5%

20. Determine the percent of profit or loss.

Gross sales	$180,000
Direct expenses	52,000
Opening inventory (at cost)	39,000
Indirect expenses	27,000
Purchases, at cost	95,000
Customer returns	8,000
Inward freight	1,000
Closing inventory (at cost)	44,000
Cash discounts	4%

*21. Your merchandise manager has pointed out that the profit percentage in your department for the most recent period was extremely poor. In conjunction with your assistant buyers, make a list of as many ways which you, as buyer, can directly attempt to improve the situation.

*22. Set up a demonstration mathematical example to show how *increased profit* percentage might be achieved in a departmental operation despite *reduced volume.* Explain.

―――――――――――――――――――――――――――――――――――――――
*For research and discussion.

23. Based on what you already know as a consumer, and in view of changing economic patterns over the last three decades, make a "Ball Park" estimate of the cost, gross margin and expense figures in the spaces below. Give a brief explanation of your estimated figures.

	1950	1960	1980
Net Sales	$1,000,000	$1,000,000	$1,000,000
– Cost of Goods	_____	_____	_____
= Gross Margin	_____	_____	_____
– Expenses	_____	_____	_____
= Profit	$ 30,000	$ 30,000	$ 30,000

48

UNIT TWO

The Retail Method of Inventory

To control and guide the operations of a retail store it is absolutely necessary to keep records. Records are the working tools that provide information for making everyday decisions. They can help to show whether the business is profitable. Records can tell the merchandiser what types of merchandise are needed, when and how much is needed. Of particular concern to management and to a buyer is the control of inventory.

Successful merchandising requires that the *size* of stocks offered the consumer be large enough to satisfy demand, yet that the *dollar investment* be kept as low as possible. This can only be accomplished by having a frequent indication of stock on hand. The retail merchandiser who is concerned with "how much can I sell?" must know how much to buy to maintain this satisfactory relationship between the amount of sales volume and the size of stocks carried.

In large retail stores, it would be prohibitively costly and inconvenient to constantly determine the value of the amount of stock on hand by taking an actual count. However, since this balance of sales to stocks is vital, a system of accounting which determines the probable amount of stock on hand at any given time without physically counting the goods has been devised. This retail system of accounting is called the RETAIL METHOD OF INVENTORY.

In the retail method of inventory, the retail stock figure at the end of an accounting period is the basis for determining the cost value of stock. It is a method of "averages." The conversion of the closing inventory at retail to a cost figure has already been illustrated in the calculation of the gross margin figure. (See *Unit I, page 26*.) To understand the retail method of inventory, it is important to realize that it operates on the theory that the merchandise in stock is always representative of the total merchandise handled (stock plus new purchases) to date. It permits one to find an acceptable *cost value* of the book inventory so that gross margin can be determined periodically.

It is common practice for large stores to "think at retail." Why?

- In the preceding chapter on profit, it was explained that retail sales, i.e., net sales (100%) are the basis for analyzing all the relationships of expenses to sales, and the ultimate determination of whether the merchandising endeavors resulted in a profit or a loss. Gross margin, which is the difference between the cost of goods sold and the income received from this merchandise (net sales) is also expressed as a percentage of net sales. Therefore, the danger of failing to make the correct percentage comparisons is eliminated since they are all calculated on the same base (net sales) which is a retail figure. The dollar value of the inventory owned must *also* be expressed as a retail figure to predetermine the desired relationship of these two factors (sales to stocks).
- In an attempt to improve the process of buying and selling in order to yield a more satisfactory profit, retailers compare their merchandising operation with that of other retailers. They compare such factors as net sales (retail figure) produced, the relationship of retail stock to net sales to attain the needed proportion, the pricing of merchandise expressed as a percentage based on the retail, and the percentage of reductions needed in revising prices originally set on merchandise.
- For the filing of income tax and insurance claims, etc., the *current* retail price of the merchandise is the significant valuation. All of this involves the maintenance of a perpetual retail inventory figure. Though inventory figures are not always perpetually derived, they can be obtained as often as is desirable, usually every week or month.

I. WHAT IS THE RETAIL METHOD OF INVENTORY?

The retail system of merchandise accounting permits the retailer to determine the value (at retail) of the stock on hand at frequent and periodic intervals without taking *constant* physical counts. However, it must be noted that periodic, generally semi-annual, physical counts (inventories) are taken at the then current retail prices of the merchandise on hand. In order to control the stocks and to determine the profitability of individual departments, the retail method of accounting is applied *separately for each department.*

The system requires data about the records pertaining to any movement of merchandise from the time it is bought until it is sold to the consumer. The retail method of inventory requires maintaining a book inventory at retail, as well as other records, that permits the *calculation of the cost of total merchandise handled* during the period. This, in turn, allows the constant calculation of the gross margin amount with the possible protection of profitability. (See *Unit I, page 26.*) All additions (dollar value) to and deductions from stock must be recorded. The computation from "statistical records" (book figures) of the amount of merchandise that should be on hand (at retail) is called a BOOK INVENTORY. At the beginning of the accounting period under consideration, a PHYSICAL INVENTORY COUNT is taken at the current retail price of the goods owned. It is common when large stores take this physical count of stocks semi-annually and record the value at retail that the SEASON LETTER (date of receipt of merchandise into stock) is also recorded. For example, Figure 2 illustrates the information generally recorded during a physical inventory count.

FIGURE 2. PHYSICAL COUNT SHEET

Under this method, it is not necessary, when taking a physical inventory, to list the cost price of each individual item. The physical count of each individual item, at the retail price stated on its ticket, is computed and the total retail figure (e.g., $100,000) is the actual amount of goods accounted for at the time the semi-annual count is made. If need be, this count can be made more often. This actual count figure, $100,000, is the figure then used as a *closing physical stock figure* for that accounting period. When this physical inventory value is *less* than the book inventory, the difference is called a SHORTAGE. When the physical inventory value *exceeds* the book inventory, that difference is called an OVERAGE.

II. GENERAL PROCEDURE IN IMPLEMENTING THE RETAIL METHOD OF INVENTORY

A. Finding an Opening Inventory Figure

When the "retail method" system is *first* installed, a complete physical count, *at retail* (see Figure 2), is taken for each merchandising department. (Bear in mind, that this is a figure reflecting the *retail* value of the goods.) The retail value of the goods counted is used as the OPENING BOOK INVENTORY figure. This is the same figure as the CLOSING PHYSICAL STOCK figure of the previous accounting period. Inventory counts continue to be taken semi-annually at the then current retail prices of the goods.

B. Maintaining a Perpetual Book Inventory Figure

During the time period between the semi-annual physical counts just described, many merchandising transactions occur. Goods are sold to customers; merchandise is purchased from resources and received; customers return merchandise; merchandise is marked down; goods are transferred to other departments in the same store for resale, or merchandise is transferred to other stores; and, occasionally, merchandise is returned to vendors. Every such transaction, and any other kind of merchandise movement is accompanied by "paper work" in the form of saleschecks, return-to-vendor forms, orders, and others. The statistical division of the retail organization records each and every transaction, and adds to or reduces the "book stock" accordingly, in the direction of the movement of merchandise. For example, sales to customers or transfers to another department reduce the "book stock" (also known as PERPETUAL or RUNNING BOOK INVENTORY) by the dollar amount corresponding to the retail value of the goods sold or transferred. The records must be current and accurate so that a retail book inventory figure is always available during an accounting period. Any *additions* to or *deductions* from stock must be recorded at the current retail prices and reported to the statistical department. (Every change that affects the *value* of the stock must be recorded.)

C. Forms Used in the Retail Method of Inventory

Today a retailer's records are often supplemented and/or obtained through its computer system, viz. P.O.S. (point-of-sale) markdowns. *How* the information is recorded is a matter of choice, but the loss of or failure to record the proper information showing the increase or decrease in the value of the stock will result in an inaccurate stock valuation of the book inventory. Each form serves a particular function, but not all retailers use identical forms. Some of the forms used to appreciate or depreciate the value of the stock are listed and illustrated below.

1. **Journal or Purchase Record**

   This form (Figure 3) provides a record of the billed or invoiced cost, transportation charges, cash discount, retail amount, and the percent of markup for each individual purchase. The names of the vendors, dates of invoices, and the invoice numbers are also entered. Each department checks this record periodically to insure being charged or credited with merchandise either entering or leaving a department, and only intended for that department.

FIGURE 3. JOURNAL OF PURCHASE RECORD

DATE 04/30							-- RETAIL PURCHASE JOURNAL --					PAGE		
ST	DEPT. NO.	VENDOR NO.	APRON NO.	INV. NO.	INV. DATE	REC. DATE	RETAIL	INV. AMT.	MU%	TRANS.	DISCOUNT	ANTIC.	VENDOR FRT.	NET
DIV 04				VENDOR NAME										
				GREEN & CO.										
2	310100	616920	14020	004805	3/01/1	3/10	115	62.10	46.00	.00	1.86	.00	.00	60.24
8	310100	616920	48049	004805	3/08/1	3/10	126	69.10	45.16	.00	2.07	.00	.00	67.03
8	310100	616920	48049	004806	3/08/1	3/10	76	41.80	45.00	.00	1.25	.00	.00	40.55
°	310100	616920	48049	004807	3/08/1	3/10	773	395.05	48.89	.00	11.85	.00	.00	383.20
2	310100	616920	14936	004984	3/16/1	3/17	360	197.87	45.04	.00	5.94	.00	.00	191.93
2	310100	616920	14936	004985	3/16/1	3/17	619	387.23	37.44	.00	11.62	.00	.00	375.61
3	310100	616920	49226	005069	3/19/1	3/22	317	174.50	44.95	.00	5.24	.00	.00	169.26
3	310100	616920	49226	005070	3/19/1	3/22	417	229.54	44.95	.00	6.89	.00	.00	222.65
2	310100	616920	AJ742	SU 074230	4/05/1			.00		.00	17.65-	.00	.00	17.65
			TOTALS FOR VENDOR	616920			2,603	1,557.19		.00	29.07	.00	.00	1,528.12

2. Transfer of Goods

A transfer of merchandise involves the movement of goods. When the merchandise leaves a department, the transfer is *out;* when the merchandise is received, the transfer is *in*. When merchandise is transferred from one store to another (branch), this form (Figure 4) is used to record the number of units transferred, the unit cost, total cost, unit retail and total retail. Merchandise may also be transferred from one department to another.

FIGURE 4. TRANSFER OF GOODS FORM

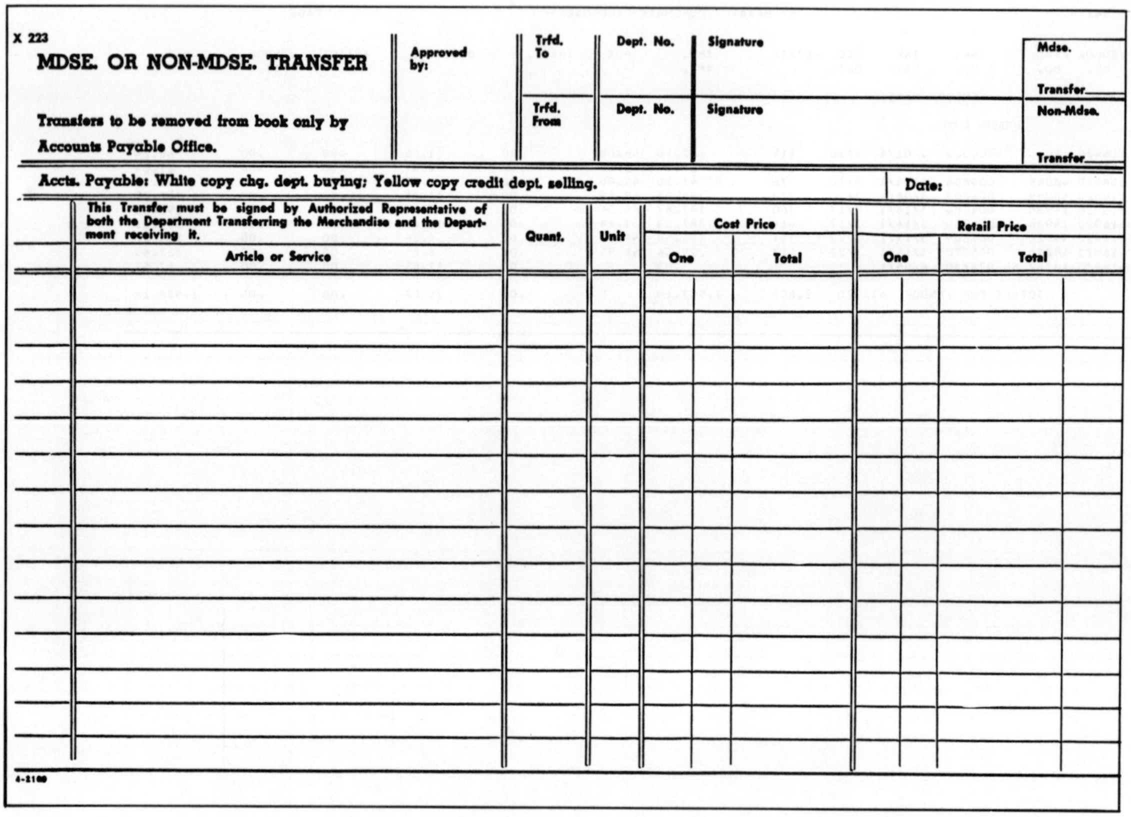

X 223

MDSE. OR NON-MDSE. TRANSFER

Approved by:

Trfd. To | Dept. No. | Signature

Trfd. From | Dept. No. | Signature

Mdse. Transfer

Non-Mdse. Transfer

Transfers to be removed from book only by Accounts Payable Office.

Accts. Payable: White copy chg. dept. buying; Yellow copy credit dept. selling.

Date:

This Transfer must be signed by Authorized Representative of both the Department Transferring the Merchandise and the Department receiving it.

Article or Service	Quant.	Unit	Cost Price One	Cost Price Total	Retail Price One	Retail Price Total

4-2100

3. Price Change Forms

All retail price changes which are required to merchandise a department must be recorded. The number of units, the old retail price per unit, the new retail price per unit, the difference per unit, and the total amount of difference are necessary. Today it is common that *temporary* price changes are recorded by a cash register at the time of the purchase. This is called a point-of-sale markdown (P.O.S.). When a consumer pays for his purchase, the new or lower retail is recorded by programming the cash register according to the prescribed reduction posted on signs displayed on the merchandise. Only *permanent* reductions are recorded on forms typical of these that follow. The following form (Figure 5) permits the listing of any or all price changes. However, some retailers require a separate form for each type of price change transaction. (Figures 6 and 7)

FIGURE 5. PRICE CHANGE FORM

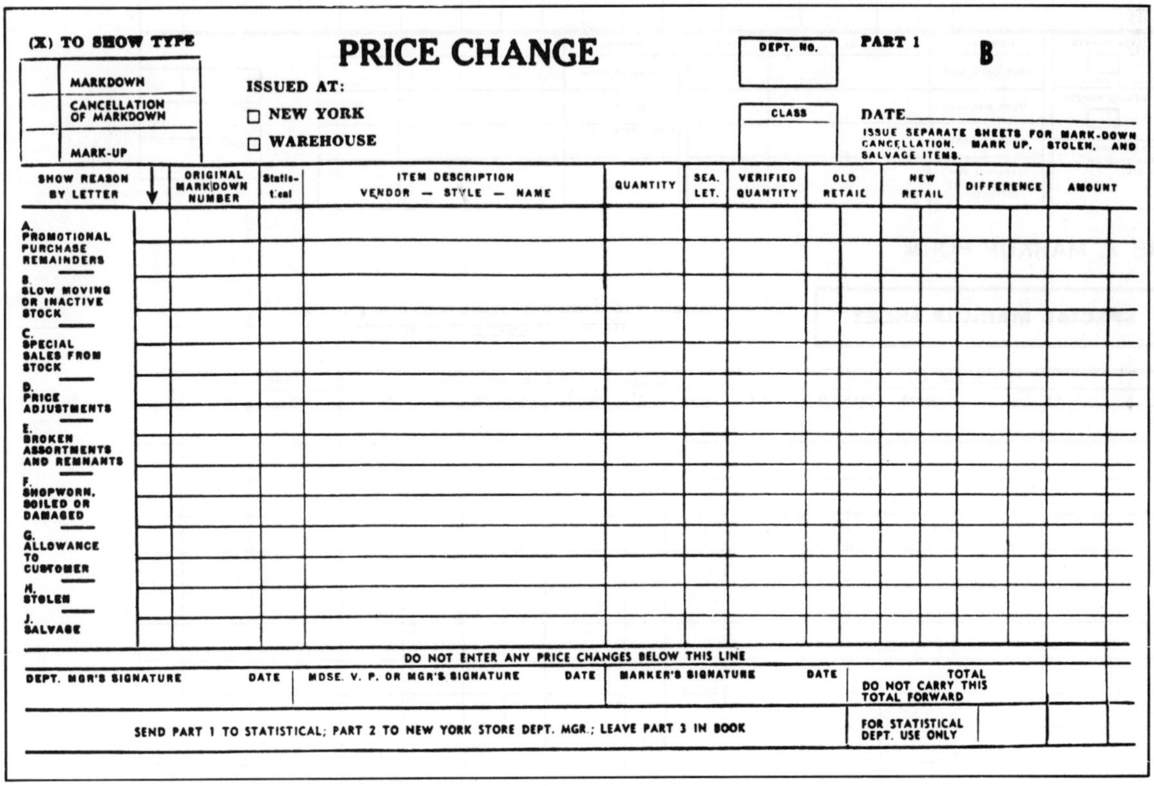
(X) TO SHOW TYPE

MARKDOWN

CANCELLATION OF MARKDOWN

MARK-UP

PRICE CHANGE

ISSUED AT:

☐ NEW YORK

☐ WAREHOUSE

DEPT. NO.

CLASS

PART 1

B

DATE

ISSUE SEPARATE SHEETS FOR MARK-DOWN CANCELLATION, MARK UP, STOLEN, AND SALVAGE ITEMS.

SHOW REASON BY LETTER	↓	ORIGINAL MARKDOWN NUMBER	Statistical	ITEM DESCRIPTION VENDOR — STYLE — NAME	QUANTITY	SEA. LET.	VERIFIED QUANTITY	OLD RETAIL	NEW RETAIL	DIFFERENCE	AMOUNT
A. PROMOTIONAL PURCHASE REMAINDERS											
B. SLOW MOVING OR INACTIVE STOCK											
C. SPECIAL SALES FROM STOCK											
D. PRICE ADJUSTMENTS											
E. BROKEN ASSORTMENTS AND REMNANTS											
F. SHOPWORN, SOILED OR DAMAGED											
G. ALLOWANCE TO CUSTOMER											
H. STOLEN											
J. SALVAGE											

DO NOT ENTER ANY PRICE CHANGES BELOW THIS LINE

DEPT. MGR'S SIGNATURE DATE | MDSE. V. P. OR MGR'S SIGNATURE DATE | MARKER'S SIGNATURE DATE | TOTAL DO NOT CARRY THIS TOTAL FORWARD

SEND PART 1 TO STATISTICAL; PART 2 TO NEW YORK STORE DEPT. MGR.; LEAVE PART 3 IN BOOK | FOR STATISTICAL DEPT. USE ONLY

FIGURE 6. MARKDOWN FORM

FIGURE 7. MARKUP FORM

4. Charge-Back to Vendors

This form records the return of merchandise from the retailer to the vendor, which may occur for a variety of reasons. It shows the number of pieces or units, the name of the item, and both cost and retail prices.

FIGURE 8. CHARGE-BACK TO VENDORS FORM

June's Department Store

SEND TO:
Firm_____
Street_____
City & State_____

CHARGE TO:
Name_____
Street_____
City & State_____

Date_____
Delivery Charges
WE pay ☐ THEY pay ☐
Via_____

Date_____
Dept._____ Store_____
Terms_____

Dept. ☐ ☐ ☐ ☐

RV

To Packers
After Merchandise has been carefully checked, tear this stub off and destroy it.

THIS IS YOUR INVOICE. Do not Destroy. No other bill will be sent. If this Merchandise is returned to us it must be rebilled referring to our Invoice Number. →

RV   **RV**

STYLE	QUAN.	DESCRIPTION	CLASS	COST PRICE	TOTAL COST PRICE
		Transportation Charges			
		TOTAL CHARGES		⟶	

UNIT RETAIL	TOTAL RETAIL

Rec'g Entry No. and date (When returned on Invoice)_____
Your Invoice No._____ Amount $_____
Reason for Return_____
Signed_____ Countersigned_____
       Dept. Manager   Mdse. Mgr.

Dept._____ Store_____
Dept. Manager Please Indicate
☐ Return On Invoice
☐ Manufacturer to send check
☐ Open Order #_____
and delivery date_____

57

5. Daily Sales Reports
This is a summary form used by the department for a "flash" (unaudited) report of daily sales. An audited sales summary is also made daily.

FIGURE 9. DAILY SALES REPORT

6. Employee Discounts
It is common practice for retail stores to allow their employees a percentage off the retail price when they make purchases for themselves. It is necessary to *record* the *difference* between the retail price and the price paid by the employee. A record of this kind of transaction is essential.

FIGURE 10. EMPLOYEE DISCOUNTS.

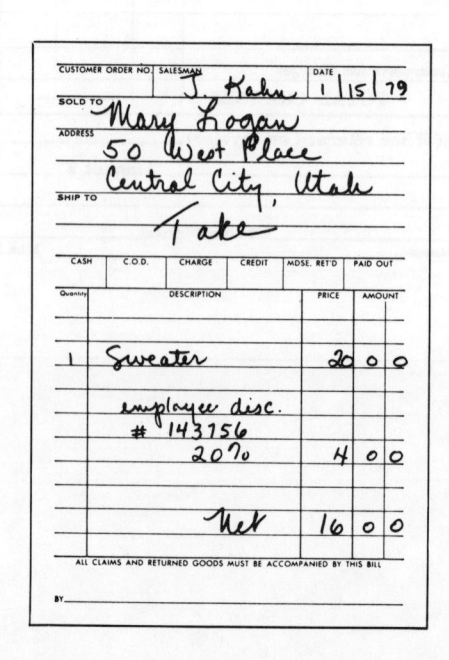

D. Calculating a Book Inventory Figure

To determine a book inventory, the subsequent steps are followed:

1. Periodically, a physical count (at retail) is taken to determine a Closing Physical Stock.

2. The physical count amount becomes the *opening* retail book inventory.

3. The opening retail book inventory is converted to a cost inventory figure by using the cumulative markup % achieved on the stock plus purchases during the previous accounting period. (See Unit I, page 26.)

4. All new purchases (plus freight on cost only) at cost and retail are added to determine the total merchandise handled at cost and retail.

5. All retail deductions (net sales, markdowns, etc.) are subtracted from the *retail* TOTAL MERCHANDISE HANDLED to find the *closing book* inventory at *retail*.

6. The closing book inventory at retail is converted to a closing book inventory at cost by determining the markup % from the difference between the total merchandise handled at retail and the total merchandise handled at cost.

    The Statistical Department constantly keeps a record of departmental purchases at both cost and retail. In addition, it continues to keep a record (at retail) of any and all movement of goods, inward and outward, as well as any transactions which increase or decrease the retail value of merchandise on hand.

    In a multi-store operation a constant inventory figure is maintained for the particular department in *each* store. This inventory figure is evaluated, not only on an individual store basis, but also on the particular department's overall operation.

    Below is an example of a department for a branch store that should serve to illustrate the "addition or deduction" of the *value* of the merchandise in stock and the careful recording of all changes in *retail value*.

EXAMPLE:

Increase of Retail Value			Decrease of Retail Value		
Purchases (total retail value of mdse. received)	=	$35,000	Net sales	=	$28,000
Transfers in	=	5,000	Transfers out	=	2,000
Total stock additions	=	$40,000	Returns to vendor	=	3,000
			Employee discounts	=	500
			Markdown differences*	=	500
			Total stock deductions	=	$34,000

*Markdown differences are included in stock deductions because they lower the value of the inventory.

Note that a "book stock" figure is based on movement of *goods*, and *not* on the movement of *money*. It can be understood, of course, that money "travels" in the opposite direction.

CONCEPT: Book Inventory at retail = The addition of the opening physical inventory figure to the net retail purchases and any other stock additions; from the resultant sum subtract the net sales, markdown differences, and any other deductions from stock.

PROBLEM: On February 1, a department has an opening retail inventory of $20,000. From Feb. 1 to July 30, it received retail purchases amounting to $40,000. The *net* sales for this period were $30,500, the markdowns taken were $2,300, employee discounts were $200, returns to vendor were $350, and transfers out were $750. What was the book inventory for this period under consideration?

SOLUTION:
Opening retail inventory (Feb. 1)	=	$20,000
Retail purchases (Feb. 1–July 30)	=	40,000
Total merchandise handled	=	$60,000 $60,000
Net sales	=	$30,500
Markdown differences	=	2,300
Employee discounts	=	200
Returns to vendor	=	350
Transfers out	=	750
Total deductions	=	$34,100 − 34,100
BOOK INVENTORY	=	$25,900

NOTES

PRACTICE PROBLEMS

1. A statistical inventory indicates an "on-hand" stock of $64,250 as of July 15. A physical count on that date reveals a stock of $62,875. What is the opening retail inventory figure for the period commencing July 16?

2. Opening inventory for a coat department is $175,000. Purchases for the ensuing six-month period are $490,000, net sales are $400,000, markdowns are $30,000, returns to vendor $10,000, transfers to third floor boutique are $15,000 and employee discounts are $6,000. Find the retail book inventory at the end of the period.

3. Using the following figures, find the closing book stock at retail.

Physical inventory January 15	$ 85,000
Purchases January 15 through July 15	165,000
Gross sales	170,000
Returns from customers	30,000
Returns to vendor	5,000
Markdowns	10,000

4. Using the following figures:

Markdowns	$ 12,000
Purchases	315,000
Returns to vendor	20,000
Transfers in	8,000
Transfers out	4,000
Net sales	265,000
Opening inventory (retail)	180,000
Opening inventory (cost)	91,800

a. What is the closing book inventory for the period at retail?
b. How would the opening retail inventory for the coming six-month period be determined?

5. a. From the following figures, determine the retail book inventory for the period under consideration.

   Opening inventory at retail $16,000
   Net sales   31,000
   Markdowns   2,000
   Purchases (retail value)   40,000

   b. Convert the closing retail inventory figure to its cost value using 49% as a markup.

6. Additional Question—Discussion: Distinguish between Physical Inventory and Statistical Inventory. Which one is more likely to be affected by human error? Why? Which one has become more accurate since the advent of E.D.P. capability?

III. SHORTAGES AND OVERAGES

Physical inventories at current retail prices are taken at the end of the accounting period. The "book stock" is now adjusted to agree with the dollar value of the physical count. Any discrepancy between the dollar value of the "book stock" and the dollar value of stock determined by the physical count of merchandise on hand is classified as a SHORTAGE (or shrinkage) or an OVERAGE. As previously pointed out, shortages exist if physical inventory is lower than book inventory, and overages exist if the physical count exceeds the statistical tally.

It is almost impossible to run a merchandising operation with 100% accuracy. Shortages or overages almost always result, and are actually expected to occur. The shortage or overage is commonly expressed as a *percent of the net sales.* The inventory shortage is fundamentally the buyer's or department manager's problem and responsibility regardless of the cause. Keeping discrepancies to a minimum is one of the challenges a merchant faces. For internal control purposes, it is sometimes desirable to estimate shortages. This *estimate* is also expressed as a *percent of net sales.* While merchandise planning is done with a certain planned shortage in mind, more often than not, the actual shortage exceeds the expected shortage.

The following shortage report, generally calculated at the end of the accounting period, shows typical shortage information. Prevention, causes and shortage remedies can then be pinpointed in a multi-store operation and an attempt to improve the shortage results can be achieved.

FIGURE 11. SHORTAGE REPORT

DIV 10 STORE	SHORTAGES IN DOLLARS CURRENT SEASON	CURRENT -1	CURRENT -2	SHORTAGES IN PERCENTS CURRENT SEASON	CURRENT -1	CURRENT -2
00						
01	8,731	2,395	3,920	2.8	0.8	1.3
06	891-	717	1,712	0.5-	0.5	1.1
09	999-	867-	1,583	0.9-	0.9-	1.5
12	293-	668	1,518	0.3-	0.8	1.6
14	5,107	507	524	5.0	0.6	0.6
15	1,056	1,361	1,928	0.8	1.2	1.6
DIV 10	12,711	4,781	11,185	1.4	0.6	1.3

A. Causes of Shortages and Overages

Shortages may stem from inaccurate recordkeeping and/or faulty physical counts. A principal contributing cause of shortage is pilferage which, realistically, can never be completely prevented. Overages can only be caused by faulty recordkeeping.

1. *Clerical errors* in calculating the book and/or physical inventory:
   - Failure to record markdowns properly
   - Incorrect "retailing" of invoices
   - Errors in charging invoices to departments
   - Errors in recording transfers
   - Errors in recording returns to vendor
   - Errors in recording physical inventory

2. *Physical merchandise losses:*
   - Theft by customers and/or employees
   - Unrecorded breakage and spoilage
   - Sales clerks' errors in recording sales
   - Overweighting
   - Borrowed merchandise
   - Lost or incorrect price tickets
   - Sampling

B. Calculating Shortages and Overages

CONCEPT: Shortage (or Overage) = Closing book inventory at retail − Physical inventory

PROBLEM: Find the dollar shortage or overage from the following figures:

Opening inventory at retail	$22,000
Retail purchases	17,500
Net sales	18,000
Markdowns	300
Employee discounts	600
Physical inventory, end of period	19,200

SOLUTION:

Opening inventory (retail)	=	$22,000	
Retail purchases	=	17,500	
Total merchandise handled	=	$39,500	$39,500
Net sales	=	$18,000	
Markdowns	=	300	
Employee discounts	=	600	
Total deductions	=	$18,900	− 18,900
Book inventory (retail)	=		$20,600
(minus) Physical inventory	=		19,200
DOLLAR SHORTAGE	=		$ 1,400

The amount of shortages or overages for a period are expressed as a percentage of the net sales for the same period.

CONCEPT: Shortage % = $\dfrac{\text{\$ Shortage}}{\text{Net sales}}$

PROBLEM: The net sales of Dept. 23 for the period under consideration are $100,000. The physical count revealed a $5,000 shortage. What was the shortage % for this period?

SOLUTION: $\dfrac{\text{\$ Shortage}}{\text{Net sales}} = \dfrac{\$5{,}000}{\$100{,}000}$

SHORTAGE % = 5%

For internal control purposes when it is desirable to estimate shortages, the estimated shortages are also expressed as a percentage of the planned net sales figure.

CONCEPT: Estimated Dollar Shortage = Estimated shortage percentage × Planned net sales.

PROBLEM: The seasonal plan for a department showed planned sales of $350,000 with a planned shortage of 2.5%. What was the planned dollar shortage?

SOLUTION:
$350,000 (net sales)
× .025 (2.5% estimated shortage)
EST. DOLLAR SHORTAGE = $ 8,750

PRACTICE PROBLEMS

1. A department showed the following figures for a six-month period:

Net Sales	$125,000
Purchases (at retail)	105,000
Opening retail inventory (Feb. 1)	64,000
Markdowns	9,000
Employee discounts	2,600
Physical count (July 31)	31,000

   a. What was the shortage in dollars?
   b. What was the shortage in percent?
   c. If the planned shortage was 2%, was the actual shortage more or less? By how much in dollars? In percent?

2. Find the shortage of overage % if:

Net sales	$137,000
Opening inventory (retail)	140,000
Markdowns	7,000
Employee discounts	1,000
Retail purchases	96,000
Closing physical inventory	89,150

3. The net sales in a department last year were $365,000. Book inventory at year end was $67,500, and the physical inventory was $66,000. What was the shortage %?

4. Find the shortage or overage % for the following:

Opening inventory (retail)	$204,000
Net sales	342,000
Vendor returns	4,000
Transfers to branches	8,000
Employee discounts	1,000
Purchases (at retail)	495,000
Markdowns	46,000
Closing physical inventory	287,000

5. If the book inventory at the close of the year is $1,500,000 at retail, and the physical inventory totals only $1,275,000, what will be the shortage %, if net sales were $15,000,000?

6. The merchandise plan for Fall shows planned sales of $35,000 and a planned shortage of .7%. What are the planned dollar shortages for Fall?

7. A new shop owner was reviewing figures with his accountant. Net sales for the first three months of business were $87,000 and the book inventory was $72,000. It was noted that the physical inventory was 2½% lower than the book inventory. Find the shortage %.

8. For the six-month period ending in January, your department showed the following figures:

Opening inventory (retail)	$262,000
Customer returns	10,000
Returns to vendor	6,200
Employee discounts	3,800
Gross sales	910,000
Retail purchases	870,000
Markdowns	30,000
Transfers in	5,100
Transfers out	4,000
Physical inventory	170,000

a. What is the percentage of employee discounts?
b. Determine overage or shortage in both dollars and %.
c. Using a 49% markup figure, convert the retail opening and closing inventories to their cost values.

NOTES

IV. AN EVALUATION OF THE RETAIL METHOD OF INVENTORY

A. Advantages

- It permits control over profit because the figures for markup (the difference between the cost and the retail of the total merchandise handled) obtained and markdowns taken (upon which gross margin realized depends) are frequently available and immediate action can be taken to protect desired profit margin.

- It simplifies the taking of physical inventory because the physical inventory is taken at retail prices. This is more easily done and is less expensive. Because all entries are made rapidly and no decoding is necessary, the personnel used does not require special training or experience.

- It provides a book inventory and, therefore, discrepancies in stock can be determined, shortage causes may be discovered, overages detected, and preventive measures taken.

- It provides an equitable basis for insurance and adjustment claims.

B. Limitations

- The most significant weakness of this method is that it is a system of averages. It does not provide a precise cost evaluation of the inventory at its present cost price. This figure (cost evaluation of inventory) is calculated by applying the markup complement percentage to the retail value of the inventory. This may result in obtaining a figure which is either greater or smaller than the invoice cost of the merchandise currently received.

- The accuracy of the system depends upon extensive record keeping.

- All price changes must be recorded.

NOTES

PRACTICE PROBLEMS FOR REVIEW OF UNIT TWO

1. The shortage in the hosiery department was $3,500. This is 5% of the department's net sales. What is the sales volume of the department?

2. In the coat department, the net sales were $225,000. The markdowns taken amounted to $15,000; employee discounts were $3,000. The retail opening inventory for this period was $75,000, and the purchases made at retail were $210,000. The buyer estimated the shortage to be approximately 2%. Determine the estimated book inventory.

3. A store with net sales of $3,500,000 estimates its shortages to be 2%. The actual dollar shortage amounted to $72,000.

    a. Was this a higher or lower percentage of shortage than anticipated? And by how much?
    b. What was the dollar difference between the estimated and the actual shortage?

4. The net sales of a department were $295,000; inventory on February 1 was $150,000; markdowns were 8% of net sales; purchases for this period were $362,000; the physical inventory taken July 31 was $188,400. Was there a shortage for this period? What was the shortage or overage % for this period?

*5. Describe fully the various methods which a merchant might use to cut down excessive departmental shortage.

---

*For research and discussion.

*6. One of the major responsibilities of any merchant is to control inventory discrepancies such as excessive shortages or overages. Prepare a brief fact sheet for new assistant buyers outlining the actions a *merchant at the departmental level* can take to effectively discharge this obligation. Briefly explain each action mentioned.

*7. Does shortage have a relationship to profit? Explain.

*8. Why might a newly appointed buyer be well advised to request that a physical inventory be taken when he takes over the department? Discuss.

---

*For research and discussion.

UNIT THREE

Retail Pricing and Repricing of Merchandise

One of the aims of every business is to yield the largest possible total profit. One of the ways a retail merchandiser attempts to secure maximum profits is through the skillful pricing of goods he offers for sale. Price is a strong motivation in consumer buying habits. It is a competitive weapon and very frequently the only way to attract customer patronage when merchandise assortments offered are comparable, if not identical. Since there are many factors that influence pricing, it can be considered an art as well as a science.

In large industrial organizations, the actual price decisions of all, or particular, products are generally the responsibility of management. In large retail stores, the actual pricing of merchandise offered for sale is determined by the individual departmental buyers or another comparable person designated by the particular organizational structure. Top management, however, does formulate the basic price policies of the store; for example, underselling its competition by 10% on all items. Although the retailer establishes the price of individual items as they are offered for sale, ultimately, *all* purchases must realize maximum profits. It must be remembered that in the final analysis, the volume of sales as an *aggregate* figure must be great enough to cover not only the costs of merchandise sold, but also the reward of profit. Pricing, therefore, is an integral part of merchandising and requires skill.

I. RETAIL PRICING

Pricing refers to PRICE-LINING, which is the practice of predetermining the retail prices at which an assortment of merchandise will be carried. A retail buyer selects and offers a merchandise assortment to the consumer at a specific price point, or PRICE LINE; e.g., $15, $20, etc.

A. The Structuring of Price Lines

A buyer creates a stock assortment by considering what price lines to carry and the depth of assortment offered at the various price points. The number of price lines, and those particular price lines in the assortments, can help reflect the desired character management wishes to project. The emphasis of a stock by price lines depends on the composition of the consumer segment that management wishes to attract. There is, however, a price structure around which buying is usually concentrated. For example, the sportswear department stocks shirts to retail for $15; this price line may cover a variety of types, fabrics and sizes. The buyer, with the proper sources of information, knows that *his* customers will pay $15 for a shirt. The sportswear department, however, may stock a variety of shirts that retail from $8 to $40. This is called its price range. PRICE RANGE refers to the spread from the lowest to the highest price line carried. Most customers generally prefer to concentrate their purchases at either one price line or several that are relatively close to each other. PRICE ZONE refers to a series of price lines that are likely to appeal to one group of the store's customers. Basically, when more than two price lines are stocked, a price zone situation exists. The price zones can be referred to as VOLUME PRICE ZONE, PROMOTIONAL PRICE ZONE and PRESTIGE PRICE ZONE. For example, when the price range is from $8 to $40, the three price zones can be illustrated as follows:

FIGURE 12. PRICE LINE STRUCTURE

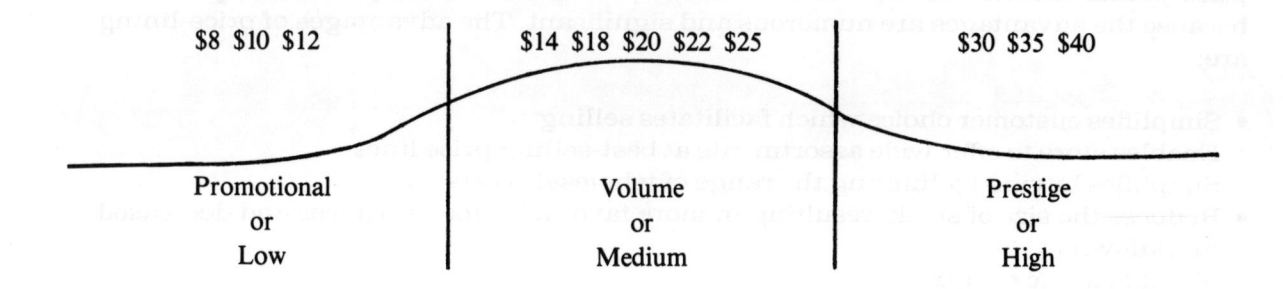

```
        $8  $10  $12        $14  $18  $20  $22  $25        $30  $35  $40

         Promotional              Volume                     Prestige
             or                     or                         or
            Low                   Medium                      High
```

The promotional price zone generally refers to the lower price lines carried; the volume price line is generally the middle price lines where the largest percent of sales occur; and the prestige price zone refers to the highest price lines carried in a department to "tone up" the assortment. This curve of distribution normally occurs within a price range, regardless of the price lines.

B. Setting Individual Retail Prices and/or Price Lines

The pricing of individual items and the establishing of price lines require experience and skill. When pricing merchandise as it is bought, one must always regard its salability in terms of its retail price, remembering that the aggregate level of all prices must be high enough to cover merchandise costs, operating expenses, a fair profit return, possible reductions, shortages, and discounts to employees. Variations in pricing occur because there are some non-controllable factors that influence pricing decisions, such as the *volatility* of ready-to-wear. The following basic factors are considered in pricing because they influence the setting of the retail price:

- Wholesale costs
- Competition
- Price maintenance policies of manufacturers; e.g., "suggested" retail prices
- Handling and selling costs
- Store policies; e.g., "loss leader" policy
- Nature of the goods; e.g., markdown risk in fashion goods
- Correlation among departments
- Demand and supply factors

C. Advantages of Price-Lining
The practice of offering merchandise for sale at a limited number of predetermined price points creates several merchandising problems, but the practice is prevalent because the advantages are numerous and significant. The advantages of price-lining are:

- Simplifies customer choice which facilitates selling
- Enables store to offer wide assortments at best-selling price lines
- Simplifies buying by limiting the range of wholesale costs
- Reduces the size of stock, resulting in more favorable stock turnover and decreased markdowns
- Simplifies stock control
- Decreases marking costs

D. Basic Pricing Factors and Their Relationship
Merchandising, the act of buying and selling, is performed by the retailer. He selects and buys merchandise which he offers for resale to the consumer. To make a profit, the retail merchandiser must set the proper price on his goods. Though the profitable pricing of individual items bought cannot always be done by applying a mathematical formula, there are three basic elements involved in the pricing of all goods. These elements are the cost of the merchandise, the retail price, and the difference between them which is referred to as MARKUP. Markup (abbreviated MU) is the amount that is added to the cost price of merchandise to arrive at a retail price. This amount must be large enough to cover the cost of the merchandise itself, expenses incurred in selling it, and the profit desired. The aim of "proper" pricing can be expressed by the following illustration:

```
         Cost of Goods
                         ⎧ Expenses
         (plus) Markup   ⎨ Markdowns, shortages, employee discounts*
                         ⎩ Profit
         ─────────────────────────────────────────────
         = RETAIL PRICE
```

Given any two of the basic pricing factors, the third can be calculated both in dollar amounts and/or in percentage relationships. The following formulas show the relationship, *in dollars,* of the three basic pricing elements.

1. **Calculating Retail When Cost and Dollar Markup Are Known**

    CONCEPT: Retail = Cost + Dollar markup

    PROBLEM: A retailer buys a shirt for $10 and has a markup of $8. What is the retail price?

    SOLUTION:
    ```
                Cost       =    $10
          (plus) Markup    =  +   8
          RETAIL PRICE     =    $18
    ```

---

*Markdowns, shortages and employee discounts must be considered in determining the original retail price set when merchandise is received into stock because they cause a reduction in *value* of total purchases.

2. Calculating Dollar Markup When Retail and Cost Are Known

CONCEPT: Dollar Markup = Retail − Cost

PROBLEM: A retailer buys a shirt for $10 and decides to price it for $16. What is the dollar markup on this item?

SOLUTION:
	Retail	=	$18
(minus)	Cost	=	− 10
	DOLLAR MARKUP	=	$ 8

3. Calculating Cost When Retail and Dollar Markup Are Known

CONCEPT: Cost = Retail − Dollar markup

PROBLEM: What is the cost of an item that retails for $18 and has a dollar markup of $8?

SOLUTION:
	Retail	=	$18
(minus)	Dollar Markup	=	− 8
	COST	=	$10

II. MARKUP

Markup, as we have defined it, applies to an individual item, a group of items, or the entire merchandise stock of a department or a store. In practice, it is the markup *percentage* that is significant (rather than the dollar amount) for comparison and analysis. Knowing the basic markup equations and their relationship to the other pricing factors aids in understanding the effect of markup on buying decisions.

A. Basic Markup Equations

Markup percentages can be figured as a percentage of the retail price or the cost price. Since the retail method of inventory is prevalent in large stores, the markup percentage figured on the retail price is more common. The cost method of calculating markup is considered to be relatively "old-fashioned," although some small retailers still adhere to this method.

1. Calculating Markup % on Retail Using the Retail Method of Inventory

CONCEPT: $\text{Markup \%} = \dfrac{\text{Dollar markup}}{\text{Retail}}$

PROBLEM: What is the markup % on an item when the markup is $8 and the retail is $18?

SOLUTION: $\text{MARKUP \%} = \dfrac{\$8 \text{ markup}}{\$16 \text{ retail}} = 44.4\%$

2. Calculating Markup % on Cost

CONCEPT: $\text{Markup \%} = \dfrac{\text{Dollar markup}}{\text{Cost}}$

PROBLEM: What is the markup % on cost, when the markup is $6 and the cost is $10?

SOLUTION: $\text{MARKUP \%} = \dfrac{\$8 \text{ (markup)}}{\$10 \text{ (cost)}} = 80\%$

(Note: Markup % calculated on cost is higher than markup % on retail.)

The retail basis is generally accepted as more desirable because all expenses and profits are also figured as a percentage of retail sales. Retailers tend to channel their planning of price lines, stocks, and customer demands in retail values, so the calculation of markup on the retail price is consistent. *Our* discussions on markup shall use the *retail basis* for all further calculations.

B. Markup Calculations Used in Buying Decisions

There are numerous purchase planning and merchandise pricing problems that face the retailer as he buys goods for resale. To achieve maximum profits, pricing is *not* done by applying the same, desirable, estimated initial markup percentage to all purchases. The astute merchandiser realizes his ultimate goal, but situations arise which may cause him to deviate as he makes individual purchases. Therefore, he is required to manipulate the combination of markup and sales volume in order to ultimately provide the largest possible dollar profit. The calculations, expressed in formulas, of the various buying and pricing situations that occur in merchandising must be known by all retail merchandisers.

1. **Calculating Markup % When Individual Cost and Individual Retail Are Known**

   CONCEPT: Markup % (on retail) = $\dfrac{\$ \text{ Markup}}{\text{Retail}}$

   PROBLEM: What is the markup % on an item which costs $6.50 and is priced at $12.75?

   SOLUTION: Given: Retail = $12.75
   Cost = $6.50

   Markup = $12.75 (retail) − $6.50 (cost)
   = $6.25

   Markup % = $\dfrac{\$6.25 \text{ (markup)}}{\$12.75 \text{ (retail)}}$

   MARKUP % = 49%

When the individual cost and the individual retail do not change, but the *number of pieces purchased varies*, the markup % is the same whether it is calculated for one piece or for the entire quantity purchased.

The following calculations illustrate this principle:

PROBLEM: What is the markup % on a purchase for 12 pieces which cost $6.50 each and are retailed at $12 each?

SOLUTION:
Total retail = $153 (12 pieces × $12.75)
(minus) Total cost = − 78 (12 pieces × $6.50)
Dollar markup on entire purchase = $ 75

Markup % = $\dfrac{\$66 \text{ (markup)}}{\$153 \text{ (retail)}}$

MARKUP % on entire purchase = 49%

83

2. **Calculating Markup % on a Group of Items with Varying Costs and/or Retail Prices**

   In the final analysis, purchases are evaluated on an *overall* basis. The following variations have the same concept which is that their markup % is calculated on the *total* amounts rather than on an individual basis so that the total purchase can be evaluated.

   CONCEPT: Markup % on entire purchase = $\dfrac{\text{Total \$ markup}}{\text{Total retail}}$

   a. **This calculation is done in writing orders placed for a variety of items and prices.**

   PROBLEM: A buyer ordered 10 coats at a cost of $59.75 each to retail for $100 each, and 6 coats costing $79.95 each to retail for $150 each. What is the markup % on this entire purchase?

   SOLUTION:

Total Retail	=	$1,900
10 pieces × $100	= $1,000.00	
6 pieces × 150	= 900.00	
	$1,900.00	
(minus) Total Cost	=	− 1,076
10 pieces × $59.75	= $ 597.50	
6 pieces × 79.75	= 478.50	
	$1,076.00	
Dollar markup on entire purchase	=	$ 824

   Markup % = $\dfrac{\$824 \text{ (Total dollar markup)}}{\$1,900 \text{ (Total retail)}}$

   MARKUP % on entire purchase = 43.4%

b. **Successful merchandising of either a classification or a group often requires varying retail prices that have the same cost.**

    PROBLEM: A buyer bought 150 handbags that cost $22.50 each. He retailed 50 pieces for $40 each, 75 pieces for $48 each, and the balance for $55 each. What is the markup % on this purchase?

    SOLUTION:

Total Retail	=	$6,975
50 pieces × $40	= $2,000	
75 pieces × $48	= $3,600	
25 pieces × $55	= $1,375	
	$6,975	
(minus) Total Cost	=	− 3,375
150 pieces × $22.50		
Dollar markup on entire purchase	=	$3,600

$$\text{Markup \%} = \frac{\$3,600 \text{ (Total dollar markup)}}{\$6,975 \text{ (Total retail)}}$$

MARKUP % on entire purchase = 51.6%

c. **Promotions are effective when merchandise with varying costs are offered at the same retail price.**

    PROBLEM: A jewelry buyer has an unadvertised promotion on rings at the special price of $25 each. The group consists of 75 pieces that cost as follows: 15 pieces cost $10.00 each, 40 pieces cost $12.50 each and 20 pieces cost $16.00 each. What is the markup % on this group?

    SOLUTION:

Total Retail	=	$1,875
75 pieces × $25		
(minus) Total Cost		
15 pieces × $10.00	= $150	
40 pieces × $12.50	= 500	
20 pieces × $16.00	= 320	
	970	−970
Dollar markup on entire group	=	$ 905

$$\text{Markup \%} = \frac{\$905 \text{ (Total dollar markup)}}{\$1,875 \text{ (Total retail)}}$$

MARKUP % on entire purchase = 48.3%

3. **Calculating Retail When Cost and Desired Markup % Are Known**
   Though cost prices can be quoted by individual or dozen prices, in pricing an item for retail, the merchandiser "thinks" in terms of *unit* retail and so uses *cost per piece* as a basis for his calculations.

   CONCEPT: $\text{Retail} = \dfrac{\text{Cost}}{100\% - \text{Markup \% (Cost complement)}}$

   PROBLEM: A top is quoted by a manufacturer as costing $42 per doz.; the markup that the buyer wants is 51.7%. At what retail price should the item be marked to obtain the desired markup?

   SOLUTION: Given: Cost = $42 per doz. = $\dfrac{42}{12}$ = $3.50 per piece

   MU% = 51.7%

   $\text{Retail} = \dfrac{\$3.50 \text{ (Cost)}}{100\% - 51.7\%}$

   $= \dfrac{\$3.50}{48.3\% \text{ (Cost complement)}}$

   $= \dfrac{\$3.50}{.483}$

   RETAIL = $7.25

4. **Calculating Cost When Retail and Markup % Are Known**
   In maintaining established price lines, a retailer who knows his required markon must be able to determine the price he can afford to pay for an item so that he can sell it profitably.

   CONCEPT: Cost = Retail × (100% − MU%)

   PROBLEM: A children's dress buyer plans to retail dresses for $10.95 with a 48% markup. What is the most he can pay for the dresses to be sold at this price line?

   SOLUTION: Given: Retail = $10.95

   MU % = 48%

   Cost = $10.95 (Retail) × (100% − 48%)
        = $10.95 × 52%
        = $10.95 × .52

   COST = $ 5.69

NOTES

PRACTICE PROBLEMS

1. Fill in the blank spaces for each of the exercises below. Note that several of the examples may be done without written calculations.

	Retail	Cost	$MU	MU%
a.	$5.00	$2.70		
b.	$14.95	$7.50		
c.	$200.00		$90.00	
d.	$1.75	$9.60/doz.		
e.	$29.95	$14.50		
f.	$10.00	$60.00/doz.		
g.		$15.00 each		48%
h.		$42.50 each		46.6%
i.		$106.00/doz.		45%
j.		$15.00/doz.		47.5%
k.	$100.00			49%
l.	$80.00			50%
m.		$16.00	$14.00	
n.		$55.00	$45.00	
o.	$75.00			52%
p.	$3.98			37.8%
q.		$21.60/doz.		46.5%
r.	$9.95	$72.00/doz.		
s.	$465.00	$235.00		
t.	$590.00	$310.00	$280.00	

2. A buyer purchases dresses at $42.50 each.

   a. At what minimum price must these dresses be marked to achieve a 52% markup?
   b. At what actual customary priceline are the dresses most likely to be marked?
   c. What would be the percentage of markup if the dresses were priced at $79.50?

3. A buyer purchased the following:

   500 Jackets costing $12 each to sell at $22 each
   700 Slacks costing $9 each to sell at $17.50 each
   300 Sweaters costing $16 each to sell at $30 each
   What is the markup % for this order?

4. Apply the following "typical" different departmental markups to find the *cost* of an item which retails for $49.95 in each department:

   a. Millinery department   54%
   b. Electrical appliances   32%
   c. Junior sportswear   50%
   d. Gifts & clocks   48%

5. A buyer of men's furnishings paid $96 per dozen for wool blend knit neckties. If his desired markup was 48%, what was the exact retail price per tie? What priceline would the buyer probably use in ticketing the ties for the selling floor?

6. If a buyer is interested in a group of closeout jackets costing $27 each and requires a markup of 49%, what would be the minimum retail price to set on the item? If the buyer had previously bought these jackets at $36 and retailed them for $65, at what markup percentage had he been operating?

7. A buyer makes a special purchase of knit shirts for a mailing piece. She buys 40 dozen at $60/dozen, 20 dozen at $72/dozen and 18 dozen at $66/dozen. If she retails all of the shirts at the same unit price, $11, what markup percent will be yielded?

8. A buyer buys straw hats at $45 per dozen and sells them at $7.50 each. What markup % is he making?

9. A toy buyer planned a special sale of dolls to retail at $25 each. He purchased 2,500 units to cover a newspaper "ad." If his overall markup on the purchase was 46%, what was his cost per doll?

10. Men's walking shorts which cost $132/dozen require a markup of 50%. The retail price of each pair should be:

11. A suit that costs $67.50 has a markup of 62.5%. What should be the retail price?

12. A buyer purchases 50 assorted leather attaché cases that cost $79.50 each. He merchandised them as follows:

    25 pieces to retail for $175 each
    10 pieces to retail for $150 each
    15 pieces to retail for $125 each
    Find the markup percentage on this purchase.

13. A raincoat buyer arranges a special purchase from a manufacturer who offers a group of 150 pieces with varying costs at one low price of $25 each. The buyer decides to price this purchase as follows:

    50 pieces are retailed at $35.95 each
    50 pieces are retailed at $45.00 each
    50 pieces are retailed at $55.00 each
    What markup % is realized on this purchase?

5. **Calculating Deviations from Aggregate Individual Markups (Averaging Markups)**

   In the actual pricing of goods, it is seldom possible to obtain the same markup on all lines of merchandise. Therefore, markups below average can be balanced by markups above average in order to realize the planned markup necessary for a profitable operation. *Averaging markups* means adjusting the proportions of goods purchased at different markups in order to achieve the desired *aggregate* markup either for an individual purchase or for a certain period. The proper cumulative markup results from effective averaging of many purchases. Basic markup formulas are applied to information given in order to calculate the figures required for solutions.

   a. **Averaging Costs When Retail and MU % Are Known**

   This merchandising technique involves *one retail price* with *two costs*. It is common to have *one* retail line which is composed of merchandise that has *variations* in wholesale costs. Therefore, the merchandiser must be able to calculate the *proportion* of merchandise at different cost amounts that can carry the same retail price, and still achieve the desired markup %. To understand this concept fully, it must be realized that the merchandiser is trying to *proportion the varying costs,* to achieve the desired markup %, because he is concerned with *aggregate* results.

PROBLEM: A sportswear buyer plans, for a special sale, to promote a $10 vest. He decides to buy 500 pieces, and wants to achieve a 48% markup. He places an order for 100 pieces which cost $6 each. What will be the average cost of the remaining pieces?

SOLUTION: (Given information is in **bold**, and the other items are calculated from the basic markup formulas; each calculation is identified with the steps of the procedure.)

Step 1: Find total planned retail. (500 pcs. × $10 = $5,000)

Step 2: Find total cost of total planned retail from planned MU%.
C = R × (100% − MU%)
C = $5,000 × (100% − 48%)
C = $5,000 × .52
C = $2,600

Step 3: Find cost of purchases to date. (100 pcs. × $6 = $600)

Step 4: Find purchase balance in units and dollars.
Purchase balance = Total planned figures minus purchases to date (500 pcs. cost $2,600) − (100 pcs. cost $600) = (400 pcs. cost $2,000)

Step 5: Find average cost of purchase balance.
Average cost of purchase balance = Purchase balance $ cost divided by purchase balance number of units
($2,000 ÷ 400 pcs. = $5)

	TOTAL PCS.	TOTAL $ COST	TOTAL $ RETAIL	MU%
TOTAL PLAN	**500** (1)	$2,600 (2)	**$5,000** (1)	**48%**
(minus) PURCHASES TO DATE	**−100** (3)	−600 (3)		
PURCHASE BALANCE	400 (4)	$2,000 (4)		

$2,000 ÷ 400 pcs.
     (5)
= $5 each for AVERAGE COST of remaining pieces

PRACTICE PROBLEMS

1. A glove buyer plans to purchase 120 dozen pairs of gloves for a pre-Easter sale. The unit retail price is planned at $17.50. Markup goal for the purchase is 48%. She buys 40 dozen pairs at the Slimline Company showroom, paying $110 per dozen.

    a. What is the most she can pay for the balance of the total purchase?
    b. What will be the average cost per dozen on the gloves yet to be purchased?

2. A sportswear buyer operates on a 51% markup. He needs 300 skirts to retail at $32 each and 180 vests to retail at $25 each. If he pays $11.75 for each vest, how much can he pay for each skirt, assuming adherence to the target markup percentage?

3. A buyer needs $10,000 worth of merchandise at retail for his department. He has already written orders for $2,875.50 at cost. His planned departmental MU% is 48%. How much (in dollars) does he have left to spend at cost?

4. A buyer plans a December promotion of 1,500 sweaters to retail at $40 each. She requires a 48.5% average markup. Her initial purchase consisted of 1,200 units costing $23 each. What is the theoretical maximum cost to be paid on each remaining unit? Comment on the buyer's "predicament" if you detect one.

5. A buyer for the exclusive Britique Shop purchased 100 cashmere cardigan sweaters at $41 each and priced them at $90 retail. He also plans to buy 72 shetland/mohair blend bulk knit pullovers to retail at $50 each. Departmental goal markup is 47%. How much can be paid for each pullover?

b. **Averaging Retail(s) When Costs and MU% Are Known**

In merchandising, a buyer must be able to manipulate markups because he may make purchases that have *two or more costs* and he wishes to determine an *average retail* which will achieve the desired markup percent, or he may make purchases that have *two or more costs* and/or *two or more retails*. These situations require the proper proportion of *varying retails* to achieve the planned markup percent because a buyer is always concerned with the *aggregate* results. The following problems illustrate the averaging processes.

PROBLEM I: At the end of the season, a bathing suit manufacturer offered a retailer merchandise which consisted of 50 suits that cost $16.75 each, 75 suits that cost $12.75 each, and 40 suits that cost $14.75 each. In evaluating the value of this offer, the buyer had to calculate the average retail price on each suit, based on his goal of obtaining a 49% markup on this purchase. What would be the average retail price of each suit?

SOLUTION: (Given information is in **bold,** and the other items are calculated from the basic markup formulas; each calculation is identified with the steps of the procedure.)

Step 1: Find total cost and total units of purchase.
  50 suits @ $16.75 = $ 837.50
  75 suits @ $12.75 = $ 956.25
  40 suits @ $14.75 = $ 590.00
  165 suits   = $2,383.75

Step 2: Find total retail from planned MU%.
  R = Cost ÷ (100% − 49%)
  R = $2,383.75 ÷ 51%
  R = $2,383.75 ÷ .51
  R = $4,674.02

Step 3: Find average retail for each piece.
  Average retail = Total retail divided by total units purchased
  ($4,674.02 ÷ 165 pcs. = $28.33)

	TOTAL PCS.	TOTAL $ COST	TOTAL $ RETAIL	MU%
TOTAL PLAN	**165** (1)	**$2,383.75** (1)	$4,674.02 (2)	**49%**

$4,674.02 ÷ 165 = $28.33 retail for each
    (3)

PROBLEM II: The suit buyer bought 50 plaid suits that cost $32.75 each and 80 check suits that cost $42.75 each. He wants a 48% overall markup. If he retails the plaid suits at $65 each, what must the average retail price for each check suit be in order to achieve his planned markup %?

98

SOLUTION: (Given information is in **bold**, and the other items are calculated from the basic markup formulas; each calculation is identified with the steps of the procedure.)

Step 1: Find total cost and total units.
  50 suits @ $32.75 = $1,637.50
  80 suits @ $42.75 = $3,420.00
  130 suits   = $5,057.50

Step 2: Find total retail from planned MU%.
  R = Cost ÷ (100% − 48%)
  R = $5,057.50 ÷ (100% − 48%)
  R = $5,057.50 ÷ 52%
  R = $5,057.50 ÷ .52
  R = $9,725.96

Step 3: Find total on established retail.
  (50 plaid suits × $65 = $3,250)

Step 4: Find purchase balance in units and dollars.
  Purchase balance = Total planned figures minus the total established retail figures
   130 pcs. @ $9,725.96
  − 50 pcs. @ $3,250.00
    80 pcs. @ $6,475.96

Step 5: Find average retail of purchase balance.
  Average retail of purchase balance = Purchase balance $ retail divided by purchase balance number of units
  ($6,475.96 ÷ 80 pcs. = $80.95)

	TOTAL PCS.	TOTAL $ COST	TOTAL $ RETAIL	MU%
TOTAL PLAN	**130** (1)	**$5,057.50** (1)	$9,725.96 (2)	**48%**
(minus) ESTABLISHED RETAIL	−50 (3)		−3,250.00 (3)	
PURCHASE BALANCE	80 (4)		$6,475.96 (4)	

$6,475.96 ÷ 80 pcs. = $80.95 each for average retail of remaining pieces (5)

PRACTICE PROBLEMS

1. A millinery buyer was offered a discontinued grouping of straw hats as follows:

   100 hats at $6.50 each
   80 hats at $6.90 each
   60 hats at $5.20 each

   Assuming she bought the lot and used a 45% markup as a guide:
   a. Find the total dollar retail of the order.
   b. Find the unit retail price if all the hats were priced identically.

2. The handbag buyer buys 60 canvas totes at $10 each. She also buys 120 print plastic totes at $4.50 each. Her planned markup is 44%. If she retails the canvas totes at $17 each, what price should she place on each plastic tote?

3. A buyer purchases a job lot of 400 pairs of men's jeans, 280 pairs costing $14 each and 120 pairs costing $9 each. If a 46% markup is targeted, what would be the average unit retail price on the lot.

4. An associate buyer for the men's sportswear classification of a college shop is shown some tropical slacks and blazers. The slacks cost $26 each, the blazers $38. Departmental markup is 49%. A purchase of 100 pairs of slacks and 60 blazers is made. If the slacks are priced at $50, which unit retail price should be placed on the jackets in order to attain the desired markup percent?

5. A buyer purchased 120 maillot swim suits at $16 cost and places a $34 retail on them. He also buys 60 string bikinis at $14 each. What would be the retail price on the bikinis if a 50% markup is desired on the combined purchase?

c. **Averaging Markup Percents When Retail and Planned MU % Are Known**
A profit goal can probably only be realized when a buyer is able to determine the markup percent he must obtain on present or future purchases to balance out the markup percent he has already achieved on past purchases. This involves the *proportioning of markup percentages* on goods so that the *aggregate* results produce the desired, planned markup percent.

PROBLEM: A buyer of coats plans to buy $5,000 (retail) worth of merchandise. He requires a 49% markup. His first purchase is 50 coats costing $31.75, which he plans to retail for $55. What markup percent should the buyer obtain on the balance of his purchases in order to attain his planned markup goal of 49%?

SOLUTION: (Given information is in **bold,** and the other items are calculated from the basic markup formulas; each calculation is identified with the steps of the procedure.)

Step 1: Find the total cost of total planned retail from planned MU%.
C = R × (100% − MU%)
C = $5,000 × (100% − 49%)
C = $5,000 × .51
C = $2,550

Step 2: Find the total cost and retail of purchases to date.
50 suits @ $31.75 = $1,587.50 total cost
50 suits @ $55 = $2,750 total retail

Step 3: Find purchase balance at cost and at retail.
Purchase balance = Total planned $ cost
and $ retail amounts minus their respective figures of purchases to date
$2,550 − $1,587.50 = $962.50
$5,000 − $2,750 = $2,250

Step 4: Find MU% on purchase balance.
$ MU = R − C
$ MU = $2,250 − $962.50
$ MU = $1,287.50
MU% = $MU ÷ R
MU% = $1,287.50 ÷ $2,250
MU% = 57.2%

	TOTAL $ COST	TOTAL $ RETAIL	MU%
TOTAL PLAN	$2,550.00 (1)	**$5,000.00**	**49%**
(minus) PURCHASES TO DATE	−**1,587.50** (2)	−**2,750.00** (2)	
PURCHASE BALANCE	$ 962.50 (3)	$2,250.00 (3)	

$1,287.50 ÷ $2,250 = 57.2% on purchase balance
(4)

NOTES

PRACTICE PROBLEMS

1. A buyer plans a purchase of coats at a 48% markup. He wishes to buy a total of $18,500 worth of goods at retail. He buys 100 coats at $69.75 each and retails them at $125 each. What markup must he now obtain on the balance of his purchases in order to achieve his desired markup?

2. A buyer needs $23,000 worth of goods at retail for May. His planned markup is 47%. On May 10, he finds that his orders to date total $5,500 at cost and $9,800 at retail. What markup must he now obtain on the balance of his purchases for May in order to achieve his planned markup for the month?

3. The buyer of a men's outerwear department needs a 46% average markup for this department and is planning to buy $9,500 worth of merchandise at retail for the month of January. He has purchased 100 imported raincoats costing $21.75 each and he plans to retail them at a 44% markup. What markup % does he need on the balance of his purchases in order to attain his average markup %?

4. A coat buyer plans sales of $75,000 at retail during April. His average markup goal is 49%. He places an order with the B&C Coat Company for April delivery in the amount of $5,975 at cost and $11,000 at retail. What markup must he make on the balance of his April purchases in order to achieve his planned markup?

5. A housewares buyer plans a $15,000 promotion of decorative stepstools to retail at $25 each at a 45% markup. He buys 500 stools from a local manufacturer for $14 each. What markup percentage must he obtain on the remainder of his planned purchase in order to reach the markup goal?

C. Types of Markup (Cumulative, Initial, Maintained)

Markup, as we have already defined it, is simply the difference between retail prices placed on merchandise, and the cost of this merchandise. We have already discussed markup calculations used in buying decisions as they relate to a single item, or a group of items. Nevertheless, the buyer is responsible for an *entire* department, and is, therefore, involved with the markups planned and obtained on the *whole* department. These markups must be constantly monitored because the desired gross margin depends on how successfully they are achieved.

To understand the different types of markup, we must clarify the term retail price. The first price placed on merchandise for resale is its original retail. The price received when it *sells*, which may be different, is its *Final Selling Price*.

1. **CUMULATIVE MARKUP** is the markup percentage generally used by retailers to compare the merchandising performance and/or information with other stores. It is this markup percentage achieved on *all* goods available for sale from the beginning of the current period. It is an *average* markup because it is the markup % obtained on the accumulated inventory at the beginning of the period under consideration *plus* the markup of all the new purchases received season-to-date. The cumulative markon in dollars is the difference between the *invoiced* cost of the merchandise (includes transportation) *before* cash discounts have been adjusted and the cumulative *original* retail prices of all merchandise handled (opening inventory + net purchases) during a given period of time. Markdowns do *not* enter into the calculation of the cumulative markup percentage. The concept would simply be stated by saying:

CONCEPT: Cumulative Markup Percent = $\dfrac{\text{Cumulative Markup Dollars}}{\text{Cumulative Retail Dollars}}$

EXAMPLE: On February 1, a boys' clothing department has an opening inventory of $200,000 at retail with markup of 49.0%.

On July 31, the new purchases season-to-date amounted to $1,350,000 at retail with a 49.9% markup. Find the cumulative markup percent achieved in this department.

SOLUTION: (Given information is in bold, and the other items are calculated from the basic markup formulas; each calculation is identified with the steps of the procedure.)

Step 1: Find the cost value of the retail opening inventory
C = R × (100% − MU %)
C = **$200,000** (100% − **49.0%**)
C = **$200,000** × .51
C = $102,00

Step 2: Find the total cost value of all purchases season-to-date
C = R × (100% − MU %)
C = **$1,350,000** (100% − **49.9%**)
C = **$1,350,000** × (.501)
C = $676,350

Step 3: Find total retail value of total merchandise handled.
$200,000 + $1,350,000 = $1,550,000

Step 4: Find total cost value of total merchandise handled
$102,000 + 676,350 = $778,350

Step 5: Find the Cumulative Markup % on total merchandise handled:
1,550,000 Cumulative Retail
−778,350 Cumulative Cost
771,650 Cumulative Markup
771,650 ÷ 1,550,000 = 49.8% Cumulative Markup %.

	COST	RETAIL	MU%
Opening Inventory	$ 102,000	**$200,000**	**49.0%**
Purchases Season-to-date	$ 676,350	**$1,350,000**	**49.9%**
Total Mdse. Handled	$ 778,350	$1,550,000	

$1,550,000 Cumulative Retail
− 778,350 Cumulative Cost
$ 771,650 Cumulative Markup

$$\text{Cumulative Markup \%} = \frac{\$771,650 \text{ Cumulative Markup}}{\$1,550,000 \text{ Total Mdse. Handled}}$$

CUMULATIVE MARKUP % = 49.8%

It should be noted that the new purchases required a *49.9%* markup to achieve a 49.8% cumulative markup, since the merchandise of the opening inventory came into the period with only a 49% markup!

2. **INITIAL MARKUP** is also known as "markon" and/or the "original" markup. Initial markup is, essentially, the difference between the billed cost of merchandise when freight charges are known, they are added to the billed cost in calculating initial markup and the *original* or *first retail* price placed on a given item or group of items. It is common practice to plan in advance an initial markup to assure a favorable *gross margin figure* that is large enough to provide a profit and satisfy expenses. It is recognized that the gross margin figure can fluctuate since it is the result of many merchandising decisions. It is also recognized that the original or initial markup placed on *new* purchases will be reduced by markdowns, shortages and employee discounts, as well as be affected by cash discounts offered retailers in the purchase of goods. These factors, therefore, in the calculation must be considered and cannot be ignored. An initial markup must be planned high enough to cover *expenses,* provide a *profit,* and also allow for price reductions that occur.

For a department, an initial markup is planned on a seasonal and annual basis, and can be calculated in either *dollar* figures or *percents* and usually both. In most large retail stores, the buyer and/or divisional merchandise manager, under the guidance and supervision of the control division, *establishes* this initial markup as a guide to check against aggregate markups obtained in actually *pricing new merchandise purchases.* One must also know that the initial markup *planned* for a season has to take into consideration the markups on the *new* purchases and their effects on the markup of the merchandise inherited from the last season, because the gross margin figure for the period depends on the markups achieved on *all the inventory available for sale.*

Therefore, to plan an initial markup, one must first *plan* probable expenses, the profit goal, probable reductions, estimated alteration costs, and anticipated sales.

An initial markup is expressed as a percentage of the aggregate *original retail prices* placed on the merchandise *not* on the prices at which they sold. This is expressed as sales plus reductions. For example, if sales are planned at $1,000,000 and all retail reductions at $150,000, the goods which eventually will be sold at $1,000,000 must be introduced into stock at $1,150,000 and the desired markup is expressed as a percentage of this total. This seasonal *planned* markup % can be calculated and *the* concept can be expressed by a formula. In the calculation of initial markup % the *basic* concept, calculated both by % and dollars can be stated as follows:

CONCEPT: Initial Markup % = $\dfrac{\text{Gross Margin \% + Reductions \%}}{100\% \text{ (Sales)} + \text{Reduction \%}}$

1. **Finding Initial MU% when GM % and Reduction % are known**

    PROBLEM: A store has a gross margin (39.3% expenses + 3% profit) of 42.3% and reductions (markdowns, shortages & employee discounts) of 15%. What is the initial markup percentage?

    SOLUTION:

    Initial MU% = $\dfrac{\begin{array}{l}42.3\% \text{ (Gross Margin \% + Expenses + Profit)}\\ + 15.0\% \text{ (Reduction \%: Markdowns,}\\ \text{shortages \& employee discounts)}\end{array}}{\text{Sales } 100\% + \text{Reduction \%}}$

    $= \dfrac{57.3\%}{115\%}$

    INITIAL MU% = 49.8%

    OR

2. **Finding Initial MU% when Gross Margin and Reductions in dollars are known.**

    PROBLEM: A store plans sales of $1,000,000, and reductions of $150,000 and requires a gross margin of $423,000 (expenses $393,000, profit $30,000.) What should be the initial markup %?

    SOLUTION: Initial MU% = $\dfrac{\$423,000 \text{ (gross margin)} + \$150,000 \text{ (reduction)}}{\$1,000,000 \text{ (sales)} + 150,000 \text{ (reductions)}}$

    $= \dfrac{\$\ 573,000}{\$1,150,000}$

    INITIAL MU% = 49.8%

3. **Finding Initial MU% when cash discounts and alteration costs are known.**

    CONCEPT: $\dfrac{\text{GM\% + Reductions\% − Cash discount\% earned + Alteration cost\%}}{\text{Sales + Reductions}}$

    PROBLEM: The desired gross margin of a store is 42.3%, the reductions are 15%; the cash discounts earned are 3%, and the alteration costs are 2%.

    SOLUTION: Initial MU% = $\dfrac{\begin{array}{l}42.3\% \text{ (Gross Margin)} + 15\% \text{ (Reduction)}\\ + 2\% \text{ (Alteration Costs)} − 3\% \text{ (Cash Discounts)}\end{array}}{100\% \text{ (Sales)} + 15\% \text{ (Reductions)}}$

    $= \dfrac{56.3}{115}$

    $= 48.95\%$

    INITIAL MU% = 49%

At this point of understanding the relationship between initial and cumulative markups, one realizes that the initial markup percent refers to those markups obtained when *pricing new merchandise purchases*. Cumulative markup percentage is the amount of markup achieved on *all the merchandise available* for sale, be it the new purchases or stock on hand at the beginning of the period. The cumulative markup percentage is the initial markup percentage calculated *from the beginning of the season* to a later date or to the end of the season and/or year.

3. MAINTAINED MARKUP

Before maintained markup is explained, it is essential to know there is a relationship between gross margin and a maintained markup, but they are not identical. *Gross margin* is the difference between *net* sales and the cost of merchandise sold adjusted by subtracting cash discounts and adding alteration/workroom costs (total cost of merchandise sold). *Maintained markup* is the difference between *net* sales and the cost of merchandise sold *without* the credits of cash discounts and with no alteration/workroom costs (gross cost of merchandise sold). Therefore, if these two factors are not considered in calculations, the gross margin and maintained markup figures would be the same. For both, the *net sales* figure reflects the *final selling prices* received for the goods sold, and the margin actually realized when the goods are sold.

Maintained markup is the markup actually achieved upon the sale of the merchandise and generally calculated for a department or when desired for a vendor analysis. It is not customary to *plan* a maintained markup because it is the *result* of merchandising activities. The initial markup *must be planned* in advance so that the desired final or maintained markup goal is achieved. It should be also noted that the *maintained* markup must be large enough to cover *expenses* and provide a *profit* while, as previously explained, the initial markup must be high enough to anticipate and also cover all possible retail reductions (markdowns, shortages, and employee discounts). One can, however, project the probable maintained markup once the initial markup and reductions are planned.

CONCEPT: Maintained MU% =
Initial MU% − [Reductions % × (100% − Initial MU%)]

PROBLEM: A department planned an initial markup of 49.8% and reductions of 15%. What is the maintained markup?

SOLUTION: Maintained MU% = 49.8% − [15% × (100% − 49.8)]
= 49.8% − [15% × 50.2%]
= 49.8% − 7.5%
MAINTAINED MU% = 42.3%

We have deliberately used the same facts when showing the calculations of initial and maintained markups so the relationship can be fully appreciated.

PRACTICE PROBLEMS

1. A buyer of lingerie determines that her department has an opening stock figure of $180,000 (retail value). This stock carries a 47% markup. On March 31st new purchases since the start of the period were $990,000 (retail value) carrying a 49% markup. Find the cumulative markup percent on merchandise handled in this department to date.

2. A department shows a gross margin (37.9% expenses + 3.1% profit) of 41% and lists reductions (markdowns, shortages, and employee discounts) of 13%. What is the initial markup percentage?

3. A small chain of specialty shops plans sales of $1,500,000 and reductions of $260,000. It needs a gross margin of $605,000 (expenses $550,000, profit $55,000). What should the initial markup % be?

4. A gross margin of 44.4% is targeted by a gift department. Reductions are 16% and cash discount earned is 4%, with alteration costs of 1%. Find initial markup %.

5. An accessories division of a large department store planned an initial markup of 51.5% and anticipated reductions of 17%. What was its maintained markup?

Unit 3B

III. REPRICING OF MERCHANDISE

The dynamic nature of merchandising makes the repricing of goods in retailing universal. Price adjustments are made to either *increase* or *decrease* the original retail price placed on merchandise. These changes in prices must be properly recorded to achieve an accurate book inventory figure used in the retail method of inventory, must be considered in planning markup goals, and must be controlled in an attempt to merchandise at a profit. The repricing of goods for sale is constant, the causes are numerous, and the skill required is considerable.

A. Markdowns

The most common and most important type of price adjustment is technically called MARKDOWN. It is the *lowering* or *reduction* in the original or previous retail price on one item or a group of items. For example, a sweater that was retailed for $15 when it was received in the store was reduced to $8.75 because it became soiled. This price adjustment is called a markdown because the retail value of the merchandise was lowered. The *difference* between the selling price and the former price is the amount by which the retail value has been lowered, and that is the significant figure to the merchandiser. The merchandiser expresses markdowns as a percentage of the net sales of all the goods during a period, month or year. Frequently, the merchandiser will want to calculate the markdown percentage that was necessary to sell a group of items, and when this occurs, it is still expressed as a percentage of the net sales figure.

1. The Purpose of Markdowns

Markdowns are "a cure not a curse." This merchandising tool can be used to good advantage if the merchandiser realizes the objectives of markdowns. The major aims of reductions are:

- To stimulate the sale of merchandise to which customers are not responding satisfactorily.
- To attract customers to stores by offering "bargains."
- To meet competitive prices.
- To provide open-to-buy money to purchase new merchandise.

2. Causes of Markdowns

By analyzing the possible causes of markdowns, a merchandiser can make an effort to minimize them. The most common causes, *not* in order of importance, are:

- Buying errors.
    - Overbuying in quantities.
    - Buying of wrong sizes (due to unbalanced buying or accepting merchandise sized contrary to order).
    - Buying of poor styles, quality, materials and colors.
    - Poor timing in ordering goods and receiving merchandise later than ordered.
- Pricing errors.
    - Poor timing of markdowns.
    - Setting initial price too high.
    - Not being competitive in price for same goods.
    - Deferring markdowns too long.
    - Calculated risks of carrying "prestige" merchandise.

- Selling errors.
    Poor stockkeeping.
    Careless handling resulting in soiled and damaged goods.
    Failure to display merchandise properly.
    Uninformed salespeople.
- Special sales from stock (off-price promotions or multiple sales, e.g., 3 for $1.00).
- Broken assortments, remnants, etc.
- Necessary price adjustments.
- Remainder from special sales.

3. **Timing of Markdowns**

Accurate timing of markdowns can help reduce the amount of markdowns needed to sell the merchandise. It is suggested that merchandise be analyzed and reduced when:

- Merchandise becomes slow selling.
- The customer demand is sufficient to sell the merchandise with a *minimum* price reduction.
- The consumer's interest in the merchandise in stock may diminish because of the appearance of a new fashion, product, or a lower price.

4. **The Amount of the Markdown**

Judgment is required in determining the price at which items can be cleared quickly. The repricing of goods is a major factor in the control of markdowns. It is difficult to generalize on the amount of the markdown to be taken because the "right" price depends on:

- The reason for reduction.
- The nature of the merchandise.
- The time of the selling season.
- The quantity on hand.
- The original markup.

Since the purpose of a markdown is to sell the merchandise quickly, the size of the markdown must be large enough to produce the desired results. The following rules can be considered in repricing:

- The *first* markdown should be sharp enough to move a considerable amount of the goods.
- Markdowns should be sufficiently large to be attractive to customers who rejected the merchandise at its original price.
- Small markdowns are ineffective.
- Merchandise can be reduced sufficiently to appeal to the next price zone customer.
- Markdowns should not be so large as to invite suspicion.
- Small, successive markdowns may *increase* the total loss.

114

5. Markdown Calculations

a. Calculating the Dollar Markdown

To find the dollar amount of markdown taken when there is a group of items, it is customary to first find the *difference per piece* between the present and new retail prices, and to determine the total "cost" of the markdown.

CONCEPT: Dollar Markdown = Original retail price − "New" retail price

PROBLEM: A buyer reduces 93 scarves from $3.50 to $2.50. What is the total markdown in dollars?

SOLUTION:
        Original or present retail = $3.50
(minus) New retail = −2.50
        Dollar markdown = $1.00 per piece

TOTAL DOLLAR MARKDOWN = 93 pieces × $1.00 = $93

However, the retailer frequently advertises markdowns as a percentage off the current retail price; for example "25% off the selling price."

CONCEPT: Dollar markdown = % off × present retail price

PROBLEM: A store advertises 25% off on a group of 50 suits currently retailed at $100 each.

SOLUTION:
Percentage off = 25%
× Dollar Retail = $100
Dollar Markdown = $25

Total Dollar Markdown = 50 pieces × $25 = $1,250

b. Calculating Markdown Percentage

For control and planning of markdowns within a store, markdowns taken are expressed as a % of the net sales for an accounting period or in evaluating a group of items and/or a particular vendor.

1. MD % for an entire department.

CONCEPT: $MD\% = \dfrac{\$ MD}{\$ Net\ sales}$

PROBLEM: Dept. #33 had net sales for March amounting to $5,000. The markdowns taken for March totaled $500. What was the markdown % for March?

SOLUTION: $MD\% = \dfrac{\$500\ Dollar\ markdown}{\$5,000\ Net\ sales}$

MARKDOWN% = 10%

2. **MD % when evaluating a group of items.**

CONCEPT: $$MD\% = \frac{\$ MD}{\text{Total dollar sales of group's final selling prices}}$$

PROBLEM: A buyer had a special selling price group of 100 snakeskin belts marked at $16 each. At the end of the season the 15 pieces that were unsold, were reduced to $10 each, and then sold out immediately. What is the MD% on this purchase?

SOLUTION: $$MD\% = \frac{\$90 \text{ Markdown } (\$16 - \$10 = \$6 \text{ MD each} \times 15 \text{ pieces})}{\$1{,}510 \text{ Net sales of group } (85 \text{ pieces} \times \$16 = 1{,}360 + 15 \text{ pieces} \times \$10 = 150)}$$

MD% = ~~9%~~ 6%

c. **Calculating Markdown Cancellation**

When the markdown price of merchandise is raised to a *higher* retail price, it is considered a cancellation of a markdown. Cancellations may occur after special sales from stock, if the remaining merchandise is *repriced upwards*. The restoration of a markdown price to the former retail is a *markdown cancellation*. Currently markdown cancellations are much less common since most large stores program temporary markdowns into the cash register as a P.O.S. (point-of-sale) markdown.

CONCEPT: Markdown Cancellation = Higher retail − Markdown price

PROBLEM: After a one-day sale, a buyer marked up to the original price of $50 the remaining 12 pieces which had been reduced to $43 for the special event. What was the amount of the markdown cancellation?

SOLUTION: Markdown Cancellation = $50 (higher retail)
 − $43 (markdown price)
 = $7 difference per piece
 = 12 pieces × $7

MARKDOWN
CANCELLATION = $84

d. Calculating Net Markdown

When a reduction in price is made originally, it is the *gross markdown*. The difference between gross markdown and markdown cancellation is called the *net markdown figure* or the amount of the permanent markdown.

CONCEPT: Net Markdown = Gross markdown − Markdown cancellation

PROBLEM: A buyer reduces 75 pieces from $50 to $43 for a one-day sale. After the sale, the remainder of the 28 pieces was marked up to the original price.
   a. What was the gross markdown in dollars?
   b. What was the markdown cancellation?
   c. Find the net markdown in dollars.

SOLUTION: Step 1. Determine gross markdown.

$$\text{Gross markdown} = \$50 - \$43 = \$7 \text{ per piece}$$
$$= 75 \text{ pcs.} \times \$7 \text{ MD}$$
$$= \$525$$

Step 2. Determine markdown cancellation.

$$\text{Markdown cancellation} = \$43 \text{ to } \$50 = \$7 \text{ per piece}$$
$$= 28 \text{ pcs.} \times \$7 \text{ MD cancellation}$$
$$= \$196$$

Step 3. Determine net markdown.

Gross Markdown	=	$525
(minus) Markdown Cancellation	= −	196
NET MARKDOWN	=	$329

117

NOTES

PRACTICE PROBLEMS

1. A suit buyer took markdowns for the month of November totaling $1,600. During this month, the net sales for the department amounted to $50,000. What was the markdown % for this month?

2. A dress buyer took markdowns in the month of July totaling $2,000. During this month, the net sales for her department were $18,000. If her original markdown plan for this month called for 12% markdowns, was her actual markdown over or under her original plan, and by how much in dollars? What was the actual markdown %?

3. The seasonal plan for a shoe department showed sales of $153,000 with planned markdowns of 6.4%.

   a. What was the planned dollar amount of markdowns?
   b. If the actual markdowns were $7,200, how did the actual percentage compare with the plan? Was the actual percentage more or less than planned? By how much?

4. A buyer reduces 75 jackets from $39.50 to $32.95 for a sale. After the sale, the remainder 30 jackets are marked up to the original price and sold at $39.50.

   a. What was the original markdown in dollars?
   b. Find the markdown cancellation in dollars.
   c. Find the net markdown taken.

5. A coat department had sales of $60,000 for the month of November. During the month, the buyer reduced 50 coats from $60 to $40 and another 100 coats from $80 to $60.

   a. What was the total dollar markdown for the month?
   b. Find the markdown % for the month.

6. A buyer had 400 pocket calculators in stock at $25 each. He marked them down to $18 each for a one day special sale. At the end of the day 210 remained unsold and were returned to the original price, at which level they all were eventually sold.

   a. What was the total markdown in dollars?
   b. What was the markdown percentage on this purchase?

B. Employee Discounts

It is common in retail stores to give its employees a reduction from a retail price. This type of retail reduction is called an EMPLOYEE DISCOUNT. We have previously noted that this is another type of price adjustment which must be recorded since it lowers the value of merchandise. This reduction is generally stated as a percentage *off the retail* price, e.g., a 20% discount. It must be recorded by the statistical department for accuracy of the book inventory figure under the retail method of inventory. The cumulative amount of employees' discounts is usually shown on the profit and loss statement under the general heading of "retail reductions."

PROBLEM: Store X grants its employees a 20% discount on all merchandise purchased. If a salesperson buys a dress which retails for $16.95, what is the amount of the employee discount in dollars? What is the amount she pays?

SOLUTION:
Retail price of dress = $16.95
Discount allowed = 20%
EMPLOYEE DISCOUNT = $16.95 × 20%
= $3.39
= $16.95 − $3.39
Employee's price = $13.56

C. Additional Markup

An ADDITIONAL MARKUP is a type of price adjustment which *raises* the price of merchandise *already in stock*. It *increases* the original retail price placed on the merchandise. It is taken *after* and *in addition to* the original markup. Though it is not a common type of adjustment, a provision must be made when it might be necessary to change *upward* the retail prices of existing inventories. An upward change of wholesale costs might necessitate the revision of retail prices to become effective immediately.

D. Markup Cancellation

MARKUP CANCELLATION is a *downward* price revision *to* the *original* price of merchandise. This type of downward price adjustment offsets the original or additional markup. It is used to adjust the markup on the purchase in accordance with the original intent, and is *not* to be used to manipulate stock values.

E. Price Change Procedures

An efficient system of reporting and recording price changes is important for three reasons: so that price adjustments can be reviewed; so that the calculation of inventory records is accurate; and so that stock shortages may be determined. Large stores practice the following price change procedures:

1. **Authorizing Price Change**

    - Buyer or person authorized by buyer.
    - Merchandise manager.

2. **Recording of Price Change**

    - Form* should indicate the old price, the new price, the quantity reduced and the reason why.
    - Recording of form by buyer or person delegated by buyer.
    - Requiring signatures on price form of buyer or person delegated by buyer, merchandise manager or marker of merchandise.

3. **Changing of Prices on Tickets**

4. **Distributing Copies**
    - One copy to statistical department.
    - One copy for department records.

F. **The Relationship of Repricing to Profit**

Every price change has an impact on gross margin and net profits. Since the elimination of price adjustments in retailing is impossible, it is necessary that stores classify each type separately so that they can be analyzed, planned and controlled. Markdowns, the major type of price changes, reduce the retail price, causing a decrease in gross margin which is further reflected in a decrease and/or elimination of profit. In certain merchandise or classifications, the markdown risk is frequently anticipated. It is offset by planning a higher initial markup. Unfortunately, profit cannot always be preplanned because there are forces in doing business which do not permit easy solutions to problems. However, it is important for the retailer to realize the effect of price adjustments on gross margin and profit as illustrated by the following example:

Initial retail value of new purchase	$ 105,000 =	100.0%
(minus) Cost of goods sold	−71,000 =	67.6%
Gross margin	$ 34,000 =	32.4%
(minus) Operating expenses	−25,000 =	23.8%
Net profit	$ 9,000 =	8.6%

The total retail reductions for the period are $5,000:

Net sales	$ 100,000 =	100.0%
(minus) Cost of goods sold	−71,000 =	71.0%
Gross margin	$ 29,000 =	29.0%
(minus) Operating expenses	−25,000 =	25.0%
Net profit	$ 4,000 =	4.0%

---

*Price change forms are shown in UNIT II.

PRACTICE PROBLEMS FOR REVIEW OF UNIT THREE

A 1. A buyer wishes to sell snowsuits at $39.95 each. His markup is 48.5%. How much can he afford to pay for each snowsuit?

A 2. If a manufacturer suggests a retail price of $12.50 for a line of tote bags costing $84.00 per dozen, what is the suggested markup %?

A 3. A manufacturer offered belts at $54 per dozen. If a buyer were to take a 47.5% markup, at what retail price would the belts sell?

4. A buyer purchased 1,500 pairs of men's lounging pajamas at $10 each for a special Father's Day sale. His "ad" price was $20 retail. He sold 1,000 pairs at the advertised sale price. After Father's Day, he integrated the remaining pieces of this special purchase into stock at $25 each. Between July 1 and Sept. 1, all but 50 pairs were sold at this price. The remainder was then cut to $12 each, and all sold at that price except 10 pairs which were too damaged and soiled to sell at any price, and therefore were salvaged.* What is the markup % on this purchase?

5. Find the markup percentage on the following handbag purchases:

   36 bags costing $22 with a retail of $45
   24 bags costing $28 with a retail of $55
   12 bags costing $41 with a retail of $75
   12 bags costing $53 with a retail of $95

---

*Goods unfit for resale and therefore reduced to zero value.

6. A job lot of 650 bow ties costs $1,950. If 400 are priced at $6 and the remainder at $7.50, what markup percentage is achieved?

7. A buyer plans to buy 250 dresses to retail for $75 each for a special sale and needs a 47% markup on the total purchase. From one of his best resources, he buys 110 dresses that cost $33.75 each, even though this markup % is less than he must ultimately achieve. He feels, however, that he will be able to average his costs on the balance of his purchases from other resources.

   a. What must the average cost per dress be on the balance of his purchases if he is to attain his planned MU%?
   b. What MU% did he get on his first purchase of 110 dresses?
   c. What MU% did the buyer have to get on the balance of his purchases in order to realize his overall needed MU?

8. A buyer wishes to buy 3,500 novelty scarves for a special import promotion. The item is to retail at $16.95 each. Planned markup is 54%. If the cost for each of 2,100 scarves is $8.75, how much may be paid for each scarf not yet purchased?

9. A luggage buyer plans a European buying trip to purchase $250,000 (cost value) of assorted travel packs. On her first stop in London she places orders for $92,000 at cost for goods, which she will price at $180,000 retail. If average markup is targeted at 52%, what markup should now be taken on the balance of her European orders?

A 10. A men's furnishings buyer purchases a closeout of 1,500 velour shirts offered at $9.85 each and 950 knit shirts at $5.80 each. His planned markup on the purchase was 49.5%. If a unit retail of $17.95 is placed on the velour shirts, what is the lowest possible retail price at which the knit shirts may be marked in order to remain within the markup framework indicated?

A 11. A buyer of sporting goods works on a 46% markup. He buys 36 sets of matched golf irons at $188 per set and retails them at $365 per set. He also buys 48 sets of matched woods at a unit cost of $138. At what retail price should the woods be sold to achieve markup plan?

12. A buyer wants $40,000 (retail) worth of men's shirts for next season. His departmental markup is 49%. He places orders for turtlenecks in the amount of $6,400 at cost and $11,000 at retail. What markup % must he now achieve on the balance of his purchases?

13. A robe buyer buys 200 cotton robes for a special promotion. She plans to mark all of them at the same retail price. Her departmental markup is 49%. If she pays $7.75 each for 150 of these robes, and $8.25 each for 50 of these robes, what retail price should be placed on each?

129

14. A lingerie department made a purchase of 100 dozen nylon briefs costing $36/dozen, 75 dozen stretch bras costing $54/dozen and 12 dozen teddies at $84/dozen. If the briefs were retailed at $6 each, and the bras at $9 each, at what retail price should the teddies be marked to attain 53% marking?

15. A piece goods buyer plans to purchase $5,000 worth of goods (retail value) during the month of November. He needs a markup of 50%. At the middle of the month, he totals his invoices at both cost and retail for the month to date and finds that his purchases to date amount to $2,000 at cost and $3,700 at retail. What markup in dollars and % must he get on the balance of his purchases?

16. A buyer needs 5,000 umbrellas for a storewide "April Showers" promotional event, to retail at $14 each. Planned markup is 49%. If he buys 3,500 units at one resource at $7.70 each, how much can he afford to pay for each of the remaining 1,500 units?

17. A buyer is offered a lot of coats consisting of 125 children's coats at $20 each and 160 children's coats at $23 each. He wishes to sell them all at the same retail price. If he is to make a 47% markup on the entire transaction, at what price must he retail each coat?

B 18. A purchase of 350 exercise bikes was made at a cost of $106 each. The item was unit priced at $200 each, and sold well at the regular price for a time. Ultimately the last 45 pieces were reduced and sold at $155 each.

   a. What was the initial markup on this purchase?
   b. What was the markdown percentage on the sale of the 350 machines?

A 19. A buyer of men's accessories purchases 10,000 neckties from a manufacturer who is relocating. The cost price is $10 per tie. Noticing that the ties are of two types, 6,200 solids and 3,800 stripes, the buyer decides to attempt some intelligent and creative merchandising. He retailed each solid tie at $18. What retail should be placed on each striped tie if an average markup of 51% is desired?

132

20. Down quilts costing $82 per unit were promoted at an advertised retail price of $160 each. Of the 800 pieces purchased, 600 sold at full price and another 140 at a one-day special mid-season sale of $125 each. Thirty-five more were cleared at $90 in the markdown corner. The five soiled counter samples were salvaged. What markup percentage was yielded on this purchase?

21. A buyer plans a purchase of coats at a 52% markup. He wishes to buy a total of $18,500 worth of goods at retail. He buys 100 coats at $69.75 each and retails them at $135.00 each. What markup must he now obtain on the balance of his purchase in order to achieve his desired average markup?

133

22. A rainwear buyer confirms an order reading as follows:
    145 tailored raincoats at $47 each cost.
     75 three-quarter length rainjackets at $26 each cost.
    If a retail price of $85 is placed on the tailored coats, and a markup average of 48% is sought, what retail price must the rainjackets carry?

23. The girlswear buyer purchases 20 dozen pairs of jeans at $108/dozen and 15 dozen flannel shirts at $96/dozen. The departmental markup is planned at 52%. If the jeans are priced at $18, what price must be put on the shirts to reach goal markup?

24. Apply the following "typical" different departmental markups to find the cost of an item in each department which retails for $69.95:

Coat department	54.0%
Shoe department	50.0%
Housewares department	46.6%
Notions department	45.0%

A

25. A blouse department took the following markdowns for November:

   160 blouses from $28 to $21
   230 blouses from $25 to $17
   170 shirts from $20 to $14
   Gross sales for the month in this department were $76,500 and customer returns totaled 6%. What was the departmental markdown percentages for the month?

B

26. For a Veteran's Day sale, a buyer reduced 95 coats from $95 each to $69 each. The following day he re-marked the 59 coats that remained to the original price.

   a. What was the amount of the markdown cancellation?
   b. What was the net markdown?

27. A buyer had 96 coats in stock at a retail price of $85 each. He marked them down to $55 for a special sale. At the end of the week, the special sale ended and 37 coats remained. The buyer marked them back to their original price. What was the net markdown?

28. A lamp retailing at $27 was reduced 33⅓%. What was the new selling price of the lamp after the markdown was taken?

29. A merchant plans to purchase $250,000 (retail value) of domestics for Spring selling, achieving, thereby, an average markup of 46%. To date she has placed the following orders:

   1,000 pillows at $9 cost to retail for $17
   2,500 summer blankets at $12 cost to retail for $22
   500 cotton spreads at $10 cost to retail for $20
   2,000 print sheets at $5 cost to retail for $9.50
   2,000 solid sheets at $4 cost to retail for $7.50
   For what markup percent should the buyer strive to complete the departmental purchase plan?

30. A buyer purchases a closeout of 1,000 coats at a cost of $46 each. He divides the coats into two groups: 425 belted coats and 575 unbelted. He decides to price the belted ones at $95 each. If his desired average markup is 49%, what retail price should he place on each of the unbelted coats?

31. A sportswear department shows an opening stock figure of $540,000 at retail, owned at a 48% markup. To date, since the last stock determination, new purchases were $1,700,000 at retail with a 50% markup. Find the cumulative markup percent on total merchandise handled in this department up to this point.

32. Gross margin in a handbag department (40% expenses + 2.7% profit) of 42.7% shows reductions (total of markdowns, shortages and employee discounts) of 14.5%. State the initial markup percentage?

33. Planned gross margin in a shoe department is 46%. Reductions are 15% and cash discount earned is 6%. Alteration costs are 2%. What is the initial markup %?

34. A menswear department planned an initial markup of 49% and reductions of 16%. Find maintained markup.

*35. "Markdowns are a normal and positive element of merchandise planning. The markdown factor may be used advantageously by a buyer in an effective departmental operation." Explain in detail.

*36. Set up a demonstration situation, with supporting figures, to illustrate how a buyer of ski parkas might take advantage of a sizeable off-season purchase to favorably influence the departmental maintained markup factor.

*37. Set up a demonstration situation, with supporting figures, to illustrate how the same buyer (see problem #36) might use an end-of-season closeout for the same purpose.

---

*For research and discussion.

UNIT FOUR

Invoice Mathematics—Terms of Sale

When retail buyers select merchandise they not only agree upon the cost price, but they negotiate other factors which influence final cost. These conditions of the sale which are agreed upon when the merchandise is purchased are called TERMS OF SALE. They deal with *discounts* granted and *dating* for payments. When the discounts granted are *deducted* from the billed cost, NET COST *remitted to the vendor* is the resultant figure. *Transportation arrangements* and *shipping charges* are also negotiated. When these shipping charges are to be paid for by the buyer, they are added to the net cost that is due the vendor, and the *final or total amount* to be sent the vendor is determined. Lack of familiarity with terms of sale is a handicap since one of the ways to improve profits is to lower the cost of goods while keeping the other factors constant. Therefore, any factor which will increase the ever-significant gross margin figure is important.

I. TERMS OF SALE

We shall examine the various types of discounts, dating and shipping terms involved in buying goods by the retailer since much of the secondary negotiating between the vendor and the retail buyer revolves around these three factors.

A. Different Types of Discount

A discount is a *deduction expressed as a percentage* from the quoted or billed cost of the merchandise granted by a vendor to a purchaser. Discount practices and schedules vary from one industry to another, from firm to firm, and within merchandise classifications. However, there are three basic *types* of discounts.

1. **Quantity Discount** is a percentage off the billed cost that is allowed by the seller of goods when a stipulated quantity is purchased. A quantity discount is deductible *regardless of when invoices are paid.* Usually the purchase of a large amount of goods is involved. Such a discount, depending on custom and practice within individual industries, is offered either when a stated quantity is purchased or for accumulated purchases over a specified period of time. The amount of discount is on a sliding scale. The larger the purchase, the greater the percentage of quantity discount. A quantity discount is an incentive to induce buyers to make commitments for large amounts of goods. This is a legal practice under specific provisions of the Robinson-Patman Act of 1936.* It is the buyer's responsibility to judge the merits of savings through this additional discount for quantity against the risks of tying up more than the normal planned amounts of purchasing power (open-to-buy). While quantity discounts are *not* customary practice in the fashion industries, they are common in home furnishings and hard goods lines.

---

*Federal legislation regulating wholesale pricing practices.

CONCEPTS: Quantity Discount = Billed cost × Quantity discount percentage
Net Cost = Billed cost − Quantity discount

PROBLEM: A cookware manufacturer has established price schedules as follows: a minimum initial order of $500 receives a 1% quantity discount (QD); an initial order of $1,250 receives 1.5%; an initial order of $2,500 receives 2%, etc. Based on this discount schedule, on an order of assorted cookware amounting to $2,000, determine:

a. the quantity discount;
b. the net cost of this order.

SOLUTION:
Quantity discount	= $2,000 × 1.5%
	= $2,000 × .015
QUANTITY DISCOUNT	= $30

Billed cost	= $2,000
(minus) Quantity discount	= − 30
NET COST	= $1,970

2. **Trade Discount** is a percentage or a series of percentages deducted from *LIST PRICE* (the theoretical retail price suggested by the manufacturer). It is a means of establishing the cost price of the goods. The number and/or amount of trade discount varies according to the classification of the purchaser, i.e., jobber, retail store, other middlemen, or industrial buyers.

EXAMPLE: A manufacturer of flashlights quotes trade discounts as follows:

Retailers (general)—35%
Department stores—40%
Chain stores   —45%
Wholesaler   —50%

Trade discounts are deducted regardless of when the invoice is paid. In merchandise lines which customarily offer trade discounts, the manufacturer is often seeking to establish a retail or *list price* for his products, and will therefore quote prices *not* at what the articles will cost the purchaser, but rather at the list (suggested retail) price less trade discount. This type of discount is quoted in some industries as a single percentage, i.e., $100 list less 45%. In others, it is quoted as a series of discounts such as $100 list less 30%, less 10%, less 5%. The clothing industries generally do not use the trade discount approach to determine the cost of an item, but usually quote cost prices directly, such as: style #332 costs $18.75 each or scarves cost $120/dozen.

CONCEPT: Billed Cost = List price − Trade discount(s)

PROBLEM: Trade discounts on a lawnmower which "lists" as $200 are 25%, 10%, 5%. Find the billed cost on an item quoted at $200 list, less 25%, 10% and 5%.

SOLUTION:

	List Price	$200	
	Less 25%	$200	$200
		×.25	− 50
		$ 50	$150
	Less 10%	−$150.00	$150.00
		×.10	− 15.00
		$ 15.00	$135.00
	Less 5%	−$135.00	$135.00
		×.05	− 6.76
		$ 6.76	$128.24
	BILLED COST	$128.24	

It should be understood that even though the list price is $100, the retailer *will not always* set the retail of the item when offered to the ultimate consumer at the suggested list price. It is common practice that the buyer uses the billed cost and the appropriate markup percent to calculate the retail price he desires.

In calculating trade discounts in series, any one of three arithmetic methods may be employed. For example, the list price of an item is $100 less 40%, less 10%.

Direct method—

$100	$100	$60	$60
× .40	− 40	× .10	− 6
$ 40.00	$ 60	$ 6.00	$54 BILLED COST

Complement method— (100% − Discount %)

$100		$60	
× .60 (complement of discount %)		× .90 (complement of discount %)	
60		$54 BILLED COST	

"On percentage" method—
.60 × .90 = .54 (Product of complements)

$100
× .54
$ 54 BILLED COST

143

3. **Cash Discount** is a stated percentage of the billed cost allowed by a vendor if payment of the invoiced amount is made within a *stipulated time*. The full utilization of cash discounts is another approach to decreasing the total cost of merchandise with a resulting increased profit potential.

Although any invoice or bill must be paid within some specified time, the intent of the cash discount is to offer the purchaser an incentive to make early payment. The vendor sacrifices a fraction of the cost due him in order to receive his money more rapidly. *Cost prices which are subject to quantity and/or trade discounts may also be the subject to cash discounts.* The eligibility for cash discount is contingent upon the *time element* only.

   a. **Calculating Net Cost When Billed Cost and Cash Discount Are Known**

   CONCEPT: Net Cost = Billed cost − Cash discount

   PROBLEM: The cost of an item is $60. Cash discount earned is 6%. What is the net cost paid to the manufacturer?

   SOLUTION: Cash discount = $60 billed cost × 6% cash discount
   = $60 × .06
   CASH DISCOUNT = $3.60

   Billed cost = $60.00
   (minus) Cash discount = − 3.60
   NET COST = $56.40 amount to be remitted

   b. **Calculating Net Cost When List Price Is Quoted and Cash Discount Is Given**
   When the cost of goods is stated by quoting a list price with a series of trade discounts, and the buyer also receives a cash discount, the amount to be paid is determined by *first determining the billed cost* and *then deducting the cash discount*.

PROBLEM: The cost of a lawnmower is $100 less 25%, less 10%, less 5%. There is a 2% cash discount offered for payment within ten days. What is the amount to be remitted if the cash discount is earned?

SOLUTION:

List Price	$200	$200	List price
Less 25%	× .25	− 50	Dollar discount
	$ 50	$150	

Less 10%	$150.00	$150.00	Intermediate price
	× .10	− 15.00	Second dollar discount
	$ 15.00	$135.00	

Less 5%	$135.00	$135.00	Second intermediate price
	× .05	− 6.76	Third dollar discount
	$ 6.76	$128.24	

Less 2% Cash Discount
$128.24   Billed cost
× .02
2.56   Cash discount

$128.24   Billed cost
− 2.56   Cash discount
NET COST $125.68   Amount remitted

c. **Calculating Net Cost Considering Quantity and Cash Discounts**
When the purchase is eligible for a quantity discount, and a cash discount is offered, the amount to be paid is calculated by first deducting the amount of the quantity discount and then deducting the cash discount.

CONCEPT: Net Cost = Billed cost − Quantity discount − Cash discount

PROBLEM: A cookware manufacturer has established price schedules as follows: minimum initial order of $500 receives 1% QD; an initial order of $1,250 receives 1.5%; an initial order of $2,500 receives 2%, etc. There is a 3% cash discount offered for payment within ten days. Based on this discount schedule, on an order of assorted cookware amounting to $2,000, what is the net cost of this order which was paid within 7 days?

SOLUTION: Quantity discount = $2,000 billed cost × 1.5% quantity discount
= $2,000 × .015
Quantity discount = $30

Cost = $2,000 billed cost − $30 quantity discount
Cost = $1,970

Cash discount = $1,970 × 3% cash discount
= $1,970 × .03
Cash discount = $59.10

Net cost = $1,970 − $59.10

NET COST = $1,910.90

B. Net Terms

Net Terms is the expression used to refer to a condition of sale whereby the cash discount is *neither offered nor permitted*. For example, an item *is sold* under a "net" arrangement.

PROBLEM: A buyer purchases an item costing $500 with net terms. The invoice is dated October 5 and the bill is paid within 30 days. What is the amount of the bill that was paid?

SOLUTION: $500 billed cost with "net terms" means no cash discount. *$500 is paid.*

NOTES

PRACTICE PROBLEMS

1. What is the net cost on an order amounting to $850, if the cash discount earned is 4%?

2. Calculate the net cost on the following order for merchandise:
   6 doz. boys' swim trunks at $84/dozen.
   Cash discount earned is 3%.

3. If a buyer purchases 120 coats at $52 each and earns an 8% cash discount, what amount must he pay to the manufacturer?

NOTES

II. DATING

DATING is an agreement whereby a specified time period for payment of an invoice is arranged. The type of dating arrangement varies within a particular industry and from one industry to another.

Dating usually implies a cash discount and is expressed as a single term of sale, e.g., 2/10. This means that the buyer will deduct a 2% cash discount from the *billed* cost *if* the payment is remitted to the manufacturer on or before the stipulated 10-day period.

For example:

Industry	Common Dating Practice
Ready-to-wear	8/10 E.O.M.
Millinery	7/10 E.O.M.
Home furnishings	2/10 net 30

Based on the third example above, 2/10 net 30 would mean that a 2% discount off the billed cost is permitted if the invoice is paid within 10 days following the date of invoice. The payment of the *net amount* (total amount of billed cost) is required between the 11th and the 30th day following the date of the invoice.

PROBLEM: An invoice, dated March 1, for 10 folding chairs at a cost of $24 each, carries terms of 2/10 net 30. If the bill is paid on any day from March 1 to March 11, 2% may be deducted. For example:

$24 ea.
× 10 quantity
$240 total cost

$240 billed cost
× .02 cash discount %
$4.80 CASH DISCOUNT

Billed Cost = $240.00
(minus) Cash Discount = − 4.80
NET COST = $235.20

However, if the bill is paid on or after March 12, the full amount of $240 is due. See below.

DATE OF INVOICE	LAST DATE FOR DISCOUNT	FIRST DATE FOR NET PAYMENT	LAST DATE FOR NET PAYMENT	PENALTY PERIOD STARTS
March 1	March 11	March 12	March 31	April 1

Discount Period (March 1–March 11)
Net Period (March 12–March 31)

A. **Different Types of Dating**
There are many different types of dating used in industry. Variations can occur within a particular industry. Generally, the nature of the goods involved influences the prevalent dating practices. For example, some segments of the apparel industry offer a relatively high cash discount (8%) to induce purchasers to take advantage of the savings inherent in early or prompt payment. This is vital in an industry composed of many small businesses which are frequently under-capitalized. From the standpoint of the purchaser (retailer) invoking the cash discount privilege, the cost of the merchandise is considerably reduced with potential implications for enhanced profit. In the determination of due dates, the buyer when paying his bills must be able to distinguish between the *discount date* and the *net payment date*. The discount date is that time by which he *may* pay in order to take advantage of the discount granted, but the net date is the date by which he *must* pay in order to attain a favorable credit rating.

1. **C.O.D. DATING** (Cash-on-delivery) is a type of dating that means payment must be made "*on the spot*" *as delivery takes place.* C.O.D. dating is generally applicable to purchasers with poor or unproven credit ratings.

    PROBLEM: Goods valued at $500 cost are purchased by a retail store under C.O.D. dating terms. What amount must be remitted? When?

    SOLUTION: Invoiced amount = $500
    Amount remitted = $500
    When = As delivery takes place

2. **Regular (or Ordinary) Dating** is one of the most common kinds of dating. The discount period is calculated from the *date of the invoice* which usually is the same date on which merchandise is shipped.

    PROBLEM: What payment should be made on an invoice for $500 dated November 16 carrying terms of 4/10 net 30?

    SOLUTION: If paid on or before November 26:

    $500 billed cost
    − 20 cash discount ($500 × 4%)
    $480 remitted

    If paid between November 27 and December 16 (20-day net payment period), no discount is permitted and the full $500 is remitted. The vendor reserves the right to charge carrying fees after the expiration of the net payment period. The exercising or bypassing of this option depends on individual cases.

3. **Extra Dating** *(written as an X)* is also calculated from the *date of the invoice, with a specified number of extra days granted during which time the discount may be taken*. Thus 2/10-60X means that the bill is payable in 10 days plus 60 extra days (a total of 70 days) from the date of the invoice in order to earn the 2% discount. The full amount is due after the expiration of the 70 days and the customary, often unstated, 20-day additional net payment period follows.

    PROBLEM: An invoice dated March 16 has a billed cost of $1,800 and terms of 3/10-60X. Determine:

        a. final date for taking cash discount;
        b. cash discount earned if bill is paid June 14;
        c. amount due if bill is paid in full on April 17;
        d. net payment date.

    SOLUTION: a. Final date for cash discount:

            March 16 through 31   = 15 days
            April (entire month)   = 30 days
            May 1 through 25   = 25 days
            END OF CASH DISCOUNT PERIOD = May 25 = 70 days
            Cash discount allowable through May 25 only.

        b. None

        c. Eligible for cash discount:
            $1,800 billed cost
          –   54 ($1,800 × 3% cash discount)
            $1,746 amount due

        d. Last date for net payment = 20 days after May 25 = June 14

4. **E.O.M. Dating** (end of month) means the cash discount period is computed from the *end of the month in which the invoice is dated* rather than from the date of the invoice itself. Thus, 8/10 E.O.M. (invoice dated April 1) means that the time for payment is calculated from the end of April, and an 8% cash discount may be taken if the bill is paid by May 10, that is, ten days *after* the end of April. Once again, a twenty-day net period occurs from May 11 through May 31 during which time the retailer may pay the bill in full.

    (Note: *Traditionally, under E.O.M. dating only,* invoices dated on or after the 25th of any month are considered to be part of the next month's transactions. A bill with 8/10 E.O.M. dated on August 26, for example, is really handled as a September 1 bill and the discount period extends to October 10. Arrangements of this kind may vary.)

    PROBLEM: An invoice for $1,000 dated March 17 has terms of 8/10 E.O.M.

        a. What is the last date for legally deducting 8% cash discount?
        b. What amount will be due if the bill is paid on that date?

    SOLUTION: a. Discount date = April 10 (ten days after end of March)

        b. $1,000 billed cost
          –   80 ($1,000 × 8% cash discount)
          $ 920 amount due

5. **R.O.G. Dating** (receipt of goods). For R.O.G. dating, the discount period is calculated *from the date the goods arrive* at the retailer's premises, rather than from the date of the invoice. This type of dating is often requested by buyers located at a considerable distance from the market or shipping point who may receive bills a few days after shipment, but who may not get delivery of the merchandise itself for a considerably longer time. Therefore, 5/10 R.O.G., for example, means that the bill must be paid within ten days after receipt of goods in order to earn the cash discount.

   PROBLEM: An invoice for $100 is dated April 4 and carries terms of 5/10 R.O.G. The goods arrive in the store on May 7.

   a. What is the last date that the discount may be deducted?
   b. How much should be remitted if payment is made on that date?

   SOLUTION: a. Add ten days to the date goods were received;
   May 7 plus 10 days = May 17
   Last day for discount = May 17

   b. Amount to be remitted on or before May 17:
   $100 billed cost
   −   5   ($100 × 5% cash discount)
   $ 95 amount due

6. **Advanced or Post Dating** (also called *seasonal discount*). For this type of dating the *invoice date is advanced so that additional time is allowed for payment* to be made and for the cash discount to be ultimately deducted. The *discount period* is then calculated from the *advanced dating agreed* upon by the buyer and the seller. This type of dating is often used by manufacturers to induce buyers to buy and/or receive goods earlier than they normally would. It is also requested by purchasers who might be momentarily short of cash. Thus, if shipment were made on February 10 and the invoice date were May 1, terms of 2/10 would mean that payment was due on May 11 or sooner with a 2% cash discount.

   PROBLEM: An invoice for merchandise shipped on August 18 is post-dated October 1 and carries terms of 3/10 net 30. When does the discount period expire?

   SOLUTION: Three percent (3%) may be deducted if payment is made on or before October 11. The full amount is due at the end of the customary net period on October 31. Note that on invoices with advanced or post dating, the payment of the invoice, at net, is delayed until the last day of the month in which the cash discount is earned, after which time it is considered overdue.

B. Net Payment Dates

Net payment dates refer to that date by which an invoice *must* be paid. It may be expressed as n/30. It is considered overdue and may be subject to an interest charge if paid *after* the net payment period. There are variations in determining the final net date of an invoice. The net payment date is *determined* by the agreed upon *type of cash discount dating*. The following are common practice:

- Regular dating—the full amount of the invoice is *due exactly 30 days from the date of invoice;*
- E.O.M., R.O.G., and extra dating—the full amount of the invoice is determined by *adding 20 days from the cash discount date;*
- Advanced or post dating—the payment of the net invoice is delayed until the *last day of the month in which the cash discount is earned.*

FIGURE 13. SUMMARY AND APPLICATION OF DISCOUNT DATES AND NET PERIOD DATES*

Type of Dating	Invoice date	Late date eligible for discount	Net amt. paid between dates below	Bill past due if paid on or later than
1. Regular (2/10 net 30)	11/16	11/26	11/27 through 12/16	12/17
2. Extra Dating (X) (3/10-90X)	6/7	9/15	9/16 through 10/5	10/6
3. End of Month (E.O.M.) (8/10 E.O.M.)	3/17	4/10	4/11 through 4/30	5/1
4. Receipt of Goods (R.O.G.) (5/10 R.O.G.; Rec'd 4/16)	4/4	4/26	4/27 through 5/16	5/17
5. Advanced or Post Dating (3/10 net 30 as of 10/1)	8/18	10/11	10/12 through 10/31	11/1

*Deadline dates are based on the actual number of days in a given month.

NOTES

PRACTICE PROBLEMS*

1. Indicate below the final dates on which a cash discount may be taken for invoices dated May 15. Merchandise is received in the store on June 2. Terms are:

   a. 8/10 net 30
   b. 2/10 E.O.M.
   c. 2/10-60X
   d. Net 30
   e. 3/10 R.O.G.

2. A retailer buys a color TV set which lists for $725 and is billed with trade discounts of 20% and 10%. Terms are net. What is the actual net cost price of the TV?

3. Your department receives an invoice dated October 10 in the amount of $6,750. How much must be paid on November 10 if terms are as follows:

   a. 10/10 net 30
   b. 10/10 E.O.M.
   c. Net

---

*All dating problems are based on the actual number of days in each calendar month.

4. Merchandise amounting to $650 at cost is shipped and invoiced on August 14. Terms are 4/10 E.O.M. Payment is made on August 26. How much should be remitted?

5. A buyer purchased 75 lamps at a list price of $40 each. The trade discounts were 30%, 20% and 5% with terms of 2/10 net 30. The lamps were shipped and billed on October 18 and were received October 22. The bill was paid on October 31. What amount was paid?

6. An invoice dated March 2 carries terms of 3/10-60X. When does the discount period expire? Explain.

7. What is the billed cost of a mini-computer listing at $1,950 less trade discounts of 35% and 10%? At what actual price would it sell if the retailer decided to apply a 48% markup?

8. If you were a buyer with an invoice amounting to $100, which set of series trade discounts would you favor? Explain.

   a. 25%, 20% and 15%
   b. 50% and 10%

9. What is the "on percentage" if the trade discounts are 30%, 10% and 5%?

10. Goods are shipped on July 1 and received on July 15. Terms are 5/10 E.O.M. The invoice is for $5,600. Payment is made on August 10. How much should be remitted?

11. Bill for $3,290 dated April 26th covering merchandise received May 19th carries terms of 8/10 E.O.M., R.O.G. It is paid on June 10th. How much is remitted? What would have been remitted had R.O.G. not been included? Why?

III. ANTICIPATION

ANTICIPATION is an *extra* discount, usually calculated at the prevailing prime rate of bank interest, often permitted by vendors when an invoice is paid prior to the end of the cash discount period. This rate is subject to change based on economic conditions. *For the purpose of illustration only,* we will use a 12% annual rate, which equates to 1% per month with a decimal equivalent of .01 per month.

The number of days of anticipation is based upon the number of days remaining between the date of actual payment of an invoice and the last date on which the *cash discount* could legitimately be taken. While some vendors do not permit an anticipation discount, alert retailers deduct it, unless a notation on the invoice expressly forbids it. Many retailers, when sending in a confirmed order, specify "anticipation allowed." Anticipation is taken by retailers because, in effect, the vendor has the use of the retailer's money ahead of the date arranged by the terms of the sale, and the retailer is, in a manner of speaking, charging the vendor "interest" for its use.* Anticipation is taken *in addition to any other discounts which may apply*. The deduction is *customarily combined* with the regular cash discount.

Currently, however, some retailers are anticipating invoices based on the number of days *from the date of payment to the end of the net period*. When using this policy, a bill paid after the cash discount period has ended can still be anticipated for the balance of the net period.

Note: In the practice problems illustrating anticipation, *only the more traditional cash discount period method should be used*. The following example, however, shows the calculations used for both the cash discount period method and the net payment period method.

PROBLEM: An invoice for $100 is dated December 4 and carries terms of 2/10–30X. Anticipation is permitted. If the bill is paid December 14:

    a. Figure the number of days that were anticipated and the remittance due using the *cash discount period method*.
    b. Figure the number of days that were anticipated and the remittance due using the *net payment period method*.

SOLUTION: a. Using the Cash Discount Period Method

The cash discount period is 40 days. Since the bill is paid in 10 days, the *anticipation period is 30 days*.
Anticipation = 1% for 30 days
Cash discount = 2%
Cash discount + anticipation combined = 2% + 1% = 3%
Total discount = $100 × .03 = $3.00
Net cost = $100 − $3.00 = $97.00
AMOUNT REMITTED = $97.00

---

*These financial maneuverings serve to undermine the role that money plays as a commodity in its own right, to be bought and sold for a fee.

b. Using the Net Payment Period Method = An alternate approach to anticipation

The cash discount period is 40 days. The net payment period is 60 days. Since the bill is paid in 10 days, the *anticipation period is 50 days*. (Note: Using the net payment period method, were this invoice paid after 40 days, i.e., after the cash discount period has elapsed, the buyer would still be allowed an anticipation discount for the 20 days remaining in the net payment period.)

Anticipation = 1.67% for 50 days
Cash discount = 2%
Cash disc. + anticipation combined = 2% + 1.67% = .02 + .0167 = 3.67%
Total discount = $100 × .0367 = $3.67
Net Cost = $100 − $3.67 = $96.33
AMOUNT REMITTED = $96.33

NOTES

PRACTICE PROBLEMS*

1. Merchandise amounting to $6,800 is shipped on March 23 and received the same day. Terms are 7/10 E.O.M. and anticipation is permitted. The bill is paid on April 10. How much should be paid?

2. Goods are invoiced on July 26 and received on August 10. Indicate the *final discount date* and the *final date for net payment* if terms are:

	Final Discount Date	Net Payment Date
a. 3/10 E.O.M.	_____	_____
b. 2/10 net 30	_____	_____
c. 2/10-30X	_____	_____
d. 8/10 E.O.M. as of Sept. 1	_____	_____
e. 8/10 E.O.M. R.O.G.	_____	_____

*In the practice problems illustrating anticipation, only the cash discount period method should be used. For the purposes of illustration, use a 12% annual rate.

3. The following goods are shipped on June 7 and received on July 2:
    50 tables at $75 list price
    200 chairs at $20 list price
   Trade discounts are 40% and 5%, with terms of 5/10 R.O.G., and anticipation is permitted. What amount must be remitted if the bill is paid on July 12?

4. On March 15, an invoice for $4,500 is received along with the merchandise it covers. Terms are 1/10 E.O.M. R.O.G. Anticipation is permitted. If the bill is paid on March 26, how much is remitted?

5. An invoice is received on April 6 carrying terms of 2/10 net 30. It is paid on April 16. What is the discount taken?

6. An invoice dated August 28 carrying terms of 4/10-90X is paid on Oct. 7. Anticipation is permitted. If the billed amount is $875, what should be the remittance?

7. An invoice for $1,800 is dated August 10. It is paid on August 20. Terms are 8/10 net 30. How much should the store's accounts payable department remit?

IV. SHIPPING TERMS

Shipping charges vary in different industries and with different situations. They are expressed as F.O.B. (free-on-board) at a designated location. The place that is designated defines the point to which the *vendor pays transportation charges* and *assumes risk of loss or damage to* the merchandise being shipped to a purchaser. The most common arrangements are:

- *F.O.B. Retailer's Premises: Vendor* pays transportation charges to the retailer's store or warehouse and, unless otherwise agreed, bears risk of loss until goods are received by the retailer.
- *F.O.B. Factory: Purchaser* pays transportation charges from factory to purchaser's premises and, unless otherwise agreed, bears the risk of loss from the time the goods leave the factory.
- *F.O.B. City or Port of Destination: Vendor* pays the transportation charges to a specified location in the city of destination and purchaser pays delivery charges from that point to his own premises. Unless otherwise agreed, risk of loss passes from seller to buyer when goods arrive at specified location in city of destination.
- *Prepaid:* Vendor pays transportation (freight) charges to the retailer's store or warehouse when the merchandise is shipped from vendor's premises. The F.O.B. agreement, made at the time of sale, ultimately determines whether the vendor or purchaser pays the freight charges.

Because the factors which determine the total cost of goods include inward freight charges, it is important that the retailer negotiate for advantageous shipping terms as a means of reducing the total cost of goods. The buyer should apply ethical but firm pressure on his merchandise resources for appropriate terms of sale and discounts.

PRACTICE PROBLEMS FOR REVIEW OF UNIT FOUR

1. What amount should be remitted to the vendor for the merchandise listed immediately below?

Quant.	Luggage Item	List Price
50	2 Suiter	$45
120	Overnighter	25
70	Dress Bag	30
90	Vacationer	60

   The bill is dated September 27 and paid on October 26. Trade discount is 45% and 5%, terms are 2/10 E.O.M., anticipation is permitted, F.O.B. retailer's warehouse. There is a quantity discount of 1% on initial orders of $6,000 or more.

2. An invoice for $4,500 was dated June 28 with terms of 6/10 E.O.M., F.O.B. store. Freight charges were $265. What amount was to be remitted if the retailer paid the bill on August 15?

3. A bill for $6,000 is dated November 8 for merchandise which is to arrive on November 25. What is the last date for taking the discount if terms are 7/10 R.O.G.?

4. An invoice for $2,300 bears terms of 2/10-30X, net 60, F.O.B. factory, anticipation permitted. The vendor prepaid shipping charges of $34. The invoice was dated August 29 and was paid on September 23. How much should the vendor have received?

5. An invoice reaches the infants' and nursery department for merchandise with a list price value of $10,750. It is dated January 28 and is paid on February 23. Terms are 2/10 E.O.M., F.O.B. store. Trade discounts are 40% and 10%. Anticipation is not forbidden. The manufacturer prepays the freight of $125.

   a. What is the last date on which a discount may be taken?
   b. What is the last date for payment without penalty?
   c. What amount should be remitted under the conditions given in this problem?

6. A sportswear buyer receives a shipment of 30 dozen pairs of pants costing $9 each. The invoice is dated April 26 and terms are 6/10 E.O.M., F.O.B. factory. No anticipation is permitted. Shipping charges of $92 are prepaid by the vendor.

   a. What is the last possible date on which a discount may be taken?
   b. If the bill was paid on May 11, how much was remitted to the vendor?

7. What amount must be remitted on an invoice for $3,200 dated April 26 and paid May 10, if terms are 8/10 E.O.M. (anticipation permitted)?

*8. If you were a small, independent dress manufacturer in a very competitive market, what terms of sale would you offer to your customers? Explain your rationale.

---

*For research and discussion.

*9. "A retailer should always exercise the cash discount option to the fullest extent." True or false? Why?

*10. Which set of terms would you choose as most advantageous to your department? The bill is dated July 16 and paid July 26. Anticipation is permitted.

   a. 5/10-30X *or* 7/10 net 30
   b. Explain your choice with supporting calculations.

*11. If you were an owner/buyer for a medium-sized specialty shop, would you always take advantage of the anticipation option when offered? Why? If not, why not? Explain your answer.

---

*For research and discussion.

UNIT FIVE

Dollar Planning and Control

Profit in retailing is determined largely by the ability to maintain a proper proportion between sales, inventories and prices. The merchandiser is responsible for providing an inventory which reflects customer demand *and* remains within the financial limits set by management. For *each* department, a sales goal *in terms of dollars* is forecast and the *size* of the inventory necessary to meet these goals is planned. The budget which coordinates sales and stocks is called a *DOLLAR MERCHANDISE PLAN*. It schedules *planned sales* month by month, the *amount of stock planned* for the beginning of each of these months, and the *planned amount of reductions*. This information permits the retail merchandiser to determine the *amount of purchases* he must make. Another essential figure of the dollar plan is the planning of a cumulative markup percentage (the difference between the cost and the original retail price of the total merchandise handled). Although the dollar merchandise plans used by different stores vary considerably as to scope and detail, sales, stocks, markdowns, purchases and markup are the minimum figures which, when properly planned and administered, should result in a satisfactory net profit for the store. This budget is prepared in advance of the selling period to which it applies. It typically covers a six month period, e.g., August 1 to January 31, and February 1 to July 31.

The chief purpose of planning purchases is to assist the buyer in making purchases at the *proper time* and in the *correct amounts* so that the stock level is in relation to sales. This plan, therefore, also provides a control called OPEN-TO-BUY. It means the dollar amount of merchandise the buyer may have *delivered* during the balance of a given period, *without exceeding the planned stock figure* at the *end* of the period under consideration.

I. SIX-MONTH SEASONAL DOLLAR PLAN

As a device for unifying merchandising operations, the dollar plan has the following *objectives:*

- To procure a net profit by providing an instrument that *plans, forecasts* and *controls* the purchase and sale of merchandise.
- To research past results in order to repeat and improve past successes and to avoid past failures.
- To integrate the various merchandising activities involved in determining the purchases necessary to achieve the estimated planned sales.

The following forms are examples of typical six-month seasonal dollar plans. Although the formats differ, there are certain common characteristics. In large stores, the statistical departments furnish the historical data. Then the buyers and the divisional merchandise managers decide upon the planned sales, stock and markdown figures from which the required planned purchases, currently referred to as *planned receipts* are calculated. It is common for the general merchandise managers and/or the controllers to be involved with a contribution to the planning function.

FIGURE 14. SIX MONTH MERCHANDISE PLAN

SALES

STORE	FEBRUARY PLAN	L Y	MARCH PLAN	L Y	APRIL PLAN	L Y	MAY PLAN	L Y	JUNE PLAN	L Y	JULY PLAN	L Y	TOTAL SEASON PLAN	L Y	STORE
01	27.8	26.5	43.9	40.4	57.6	55.0	79.0	75.5	46.1	43.5	26.8	25.4	281.2	266.3	01
02	43.8	42.3	59.5	55.8	84.1	81.3	120.1	116.0	61.2	58.4	39.2	37.9	407.9	391.7	02
03	44.3	42.8	56.7	53.6	84.7	81.8	123.2	118.9	69.3	65.7	43.8	42.4	422.0	405.3	03
05	14.9	14.1	23.8	22.2	33.2	31.7	48.8	46.6	27.5	26.3	15.6	15.0	163.8	155.9	05
07	10.8	10.5	15.0	14.3	18.6	18.1	29.3	28.3	17.7	17.1	9.8	9.4	101.2	97.7	07
08	18.8	18.1	32.1	30.3	39.1	37.7	59.4	57.2	33.9	32.6	20.3	19.4	203.6	195.3	08
09	10.8	10.3	13.9	12.9	19.0	18.2	31.9	30.5	20.3	19.3	11.0	10.5	106.9	101.7	09
12	23.3	22.2	27.3	25.5	47.4	43.8	77.5	72.0	44.5	41.3	31.1	28.9	251.1	233.7	12
13	28.0	26.2	34.1	31.6	60.1	56.1	96.3	89.7	52.8	49.4	31.2	29.1	302.5	282.1	13
14	7.3	6.6	8.4	7.5	10.5	9.5	21.8	19.5	13.3	12.0	6.5	5.9	67.8	61.0	14
15	10.1	8.7	12.5	10.4	20.2	16.9	35.6	30.7	24.9	22.2	16.1	14.6	119.4	103.5	15
16	17.2	15.8	21.5	19.5	32.1	29.5	52.8	48.2	30.2	27.9	17.3	15.9	171.1	156.8	16
17	1.4	1.4	2.2	2.2	3.7	3.6	5.8	5.7	4.3	4.2	4.1	4.0	21.5	21.1	17
18	12.0	11.2	15.1	13.7	24.9	23.3	43.9	40.1	18.4	17.0	15.2	14.0	129.5	119.3	18
19	14.3	13.6	16.9	15.6	23.0	21.7	40.3	38.0	25.5	24.0	14.7	13.8	134.7	126.7	19
20	10.8	9.7	14.6	12.9	14.4	13.4	34.5	31.4	23.7	21.6	10.9	10.0	108.9	99.0	20
21	6.1	5.5	11.6	10.2	8.9	8.3	17.9	16.3	17.0	15.5	9.9	9.0	71.4	64.8	21
TOT	301.7	285.5	409.1	378.6	581.5	549.9	918.1	864.6	530.6	498.0	323.5	305.2	3064.5	2881.8	TOT

STOCK

01	58.0	42.8	72.0	50.1	88.0	73.4	116.0	99.2	80.0	77.7	72.0	59.8	69.0	51.6	01
02	94.0	95.5	99.0	70.6	121.0	94.8	159.0	152.3	110.0	106.6	99.0	87.3	95.0	63.1	02
03	79.0	73.3	108.0	63.5	132.0	110.0	174.0	169.6	120.0	146.9	108.0	105.9	102.2	73.1	03
05	36.0	24.3	54.0	37.6	66.0	49.6	87.0	41.8	60.0	46.0	54.0	30.3	51.0	25.0	05
07	29.0	19.5	36.0	29.4	44.0	42.0	58.0	39.4	40.0	38.5	36.0	31.4	27.0	20.9	07
08	44.0	31.3	63.0	33.8	77.0	49.7	102.0	56.7	70.0	47.7	63.0	48.9	58.0	35.5	08
09	29.0	23.0	45.0	30.5	55.0	48.6	73.0	44.5	50.0	53.8	45.0	36.2	43.0	20.3	09
12	65.0	49.3	76.0	42.6	94.0	70.5	123.0	115.0	85.0	87.5	77.0	47.9	74.0	40.0	12
13	72.0	53.0	81.0	50.0	99.0	67.1	130.0	107.7	90.0	72.7	81.0	60.0	77.0	54.7	13
14	15.0	12.2	27.0	21.6	33.0	21.2	44.0	24.3	30.0	25.5	27.0	26.2	26.0	16.9	14
15	33.0	18.1	41.0	25.8	49.0	38.1	65.0	40.9	45.0	49.7	40.0	37.1	38.0	29.2	15
16	44.0	34.3	54.0	35.5	66.0	53.1	87.0	73.9	60.0	63.7	54.0	49.0	52.0	43.2	16
17	7.0	8.6	9.0	11.0	11.0	13.8	15.0	21.5	10.0	16.8	9.0	13.7	9.0	5.7	17
18	33.0	25.3	41.0	39.7	50.0	50.4	65.0	63.9	45.0	59.8	41.0	42.5	39.0	31.7	18
19	40.0	26.0	40.0	33.5	49.0	46.1	65.0	69.7	45.0	71.9	40.0	38.4	39.0	33.8	19
20	29.0	24.0	32.0	31.4	39.0	43.6	51.0	51.5	35.0	50.3	32.0	35.9	30.0	31.8	20
21	18.0	12.8	22.0	37.1	27.0	35.8	36.0	28.2	25.0	38.6	22.0	26.8	21.0	15.8	21
TOT	725.0	573.3	900.0	643.7	1100.0	907.8	1450.0	1200.1	1000.0	1053.7	900.0	777.3	850.0	592.3	TOT

PL. RCPTS.	476.7		609.1		931.5		468.1		430.6		273.5		3189.5	PL. RCPTS.
*MD	125.0	126.3	70.0	52.0	113.0	117.2	285.0	264.6	172.0	195.6	45.0	32.3	810.0 788.0	*MD

TOTAL SEASON	PLAN	L Y		PLAN	L Y	DEPT. NUMBER:
MARKUP %	58.0	57.4	GM & DISC %	50.6	49.9	DEPT. NAME: MS. BUDGET COORDINATES
MD & ED %	26.9	27.8	TURNOVER	3.1	3.5	BUYER:

*(EXCLUDING ED)

FIGURE 15. WORKSHEET FOR MERCHANDISE PLAN

$(000)

SALES ($)	FEB.	MARCH	APRIL	MAY	JUNE	JULY	SPRING	AUG.	SEPT.	OCT.	NOV.	DEC.	JAN.	FALL	ANNUAL
86 PLAN							20500								
85 ACT.	1817	3396	3476	3066	3041	2070	16865	2303						2303	19168
85 PLAN	1643	3265	3207	3238	3034	1608	15996	2231	4095	3071	3161	4233	1681	18471	34467
84 ACT.	1427	2619	2550	2701	2742	1438	13478	1766	3157	2322	2112	3077	1457	13891	27368
83 ACT.	1224	2250	2065	2366	2447	1379	11730	1725	2536	1842	1847	2620	959	11530	23260
82 ACT.	1115	2018	1947	1977	1951	1170	10177	1451	2159	1412	1377	1988	833	9221	19399

SALES % CHG.	FEB.	MARCH	APRIL	MAY	JUNE	JULY	SPRING	AUG.	SEPT.	OCT.	NOV.	DEC.	JAN.	FALL	ANNUAL
86P/85A															
85A/84A	27.3	29.6	36.3	13.5	10.9	43.9	25.1	30.4	-100.0	-100.0	-100.0	-100.0	-100.0	-83.4	-30.0
85P/84A	15.1	24.7	25.8	19.9	10.6	11.9	18.7	26.3	29.7	32.3	49.7	37.6	15.3	33.0	25.9
84A/83A	16.6	16.4	23.5	14.2	12.1	4.3	14.9	2.4	24.5	26.0	14.3	17.4	52.0	20.5	17.7
83A/82A	9.8	11.5	6.1	19.7	25.4	17.9	15.3	18.9	17.5	30.4	34.1	31.8	15.1	25.0	19.9

EOM STOCK	FEB.	MARCH	APRIL	MAY	JUNE	JULY	AVG. SPRING	AUG.	SEPT.	OCT.	NOV.	DEC.	JAN.	AVG. FALL	AVG. ANNUAL
86 PLAN							10513								
85 ACT.	7449	9578	9714	8979	8518	7581	8337	10555							
85 PLAN	8971	9703	9586	8712	7410	6950	8241	11613	12270	11810	11256	9000	8431	10190	9390
84 ACT.	7204	8802	9009	8225	6474	6105	7339	7577	8098	8536	8138	5959	6538	7279	7401
83 ACT.	5389	5986	6182	6056	5261	5140	5477	6122	6120	6460	6692	5368	5551	5922	5742
82 ACT.	5349	6188	5614	4691	4069	4481	4916	4578	5285	5031	4998	4057	4323	4679	4822

EOM - WKS OF SUPPLY	FEB.	MARCH	APRIL	MAY	JUNE	JULY	TURNOVER SPRING	AUG.	SEPT.	OCT.	NOV.	DEC.	JAN.	T.O. FALL	T.O. ANNUAL
86 PLAN							1.95								
85 ACT.	9.8	13.0	15.7	14.9	13.1	10.5	2.02	13.3							
85 PLAN	12.1	13.6	16.1	15.2	12.4	9.8	1.94	14.5	17.3	18.1	17.7	14.9	12.1	1.81	3.67
84 ACT.	12.0	15.2	17.6	16.6	13.2	11.0	1.84	13.0	15.0	18.1	16.6	13.0	10.5	1.91	3.70
83 ACT.	10.8	11.2	13.0	14.0	12.3	10.9	2.14	12.8	12.6	15.9	16.2	13.6	11.4	1.95	4.05
82 ACT.	11.8	14.1	14.4	13.3	11.4	11.5	2.07	11.9	15.4	15.7	15.1	12.4	10.6	1.97	4.02

NET RECEIPTS	FEB.	MARCH	APRIL	MAY	JUNE	JULY	SPRING	AUG.	SEPT.	OCT.	NOV.	DEC.	JAN.	FALL	ANNUAL
86 PLAN															
85 ACT.	2728	5525	3611	2331	2580	1133	17909	5276						5276	23185
85 PLAN															
84 ACT.	3080	4217	2756	1918	992	1069	14032	3238	3677	2760	1714	898	2036	14323	28355
83 ACT.	2290	2846	2261	2240	1652	1258	12547	2707	2534	2183	2079	1296	1142	11942	24489
82 ACT.	2442	2857	1373	1054	1330	1581	10637	1549	2866	1158	1345	1047	1099	9064	19700

MARKDOWN $	FEB.	MARCH	APRIL	MAY	JUNE	JULY	SPRING	AUG.	SEPT.	OCT.	NOV.	DEC.	JAN.	FALL	ANNUAL
86 PLAN															
85 ACT.	395	380	456	773	797	448	3249	452						452	3700
85 PLAN															
84 ACT.	165	533	342	628	743	122	2533	314	488	479	578	996	31	2885	5418
83 ACT.	250	233	294	228	649	162	1816	253	365	489	362	1002	90	2560	4376
82 ACT.	216	216	350	252	504	292	1830	168	223	315	366	450	204	1725	3555

MARKDOWN%	FEB.	MARCH	APRIL	MAY	JUNE	JULY	SPRING	AUG.	SEPT.	OCT.	NOV.	DEC.	JAN.	FALL	ANNUAL
86 PLAN															
85 ACT.	21.7	11.2	13.1	25.2	26.2	21.6	19.3	19.6						19.6	19.3
85 PLAN															
84 ACT.	11.6	20.3	13.4	23.2	27.1	8.5	18.8	17.8	15.5	20.6	27.4	32.4	2.1	20.8	19.8
83 ACT.	20.4	10.3	14.3	9.6	26.5	11.7	15.5	14.7	14.4	26.6	19.6	38.2	9.4	22.2	19.8
82 ACT.	19.4	10.7	18.0	12.8	25.8	25.0	18.0	11.5	10.3	22.3	26.6	22.6	24.5	18.7	18.3

A13 - RTW C DRESSES

A13 - RTW C DRESSES

FIGURE 16. MERCHANDISE PLAN

MD-GP-SALES-NEAREST HUNDREDS $
STOCK-NEAREST THOUSANDS $
SP WORKSHEET

		AUGUST SALES BOM STOCK	SEPTEMBER SALES BOM STOCK	OCTOBER SALES BOM STOCK	NOVEMBER SALES BOM STOCK	DECEMBER SALES BOM STOCK	JANUARY SALES BOM STOCK	SEASON SALES AVER STOCK	FEBRUARY SEASON BOM T.O. STOCK
CHAIN	LY PLAN	365.8 576	348.8 790	306.4 704	376.5 612	310.0 607	130.9 278	1836.4 595	3.09 321
T.O.	LY PLAN	.63	1.04	1.48	2.08	2.59	3.09	3.09	
O.T.B.	LY PLAN								
M.D.$	LY PLAN	64.8	46.3	37.8	70.8	59.2	75.1	354.0	
M.D.%	LY PLAN	17.72	13.36	12.33	18.80	19.10	57.40	19.28	
MU: PUR	LY PLAN	50.40	49.73	48.80	50.07	44.64	48.61	49.64	
MU% S&P	LY PLAN	50.12	49.69	49.20	49.49	49.26	49.07	49.07	
SHORT%	LY PLAN	2.07	2.04	2.08	2.18	2.15	2.18	2.11	
G.P.$	LY PLAN	147.2	143.6	124.3	149.9	115.5	20.6	701.0	
G.P.%	LY PLAN	40.24	41.40	40.55	39.80	37.25	15.76	38.17	
BEG SEAS MU% STK	LY PLAN	49.80							

174

A. The Procedure, by Element, of Dollar Planning

The real value of dollar planning as a guide to merchandising is that the *figures* projected *for each element* reflect goals that are *reasonably attainable*. The buyer should be involved in the preparation of the figures since he is responsible for interpreting and achieving them. He will then be more inclined to *use* the set guide lines he has helped formulate. Once completed, a *sound* dollar plan must be *adjusted* to actual conditions and results *during* the season under consideration.

1. Planning Sales

The planning of this figure is the *most* significant, and the *first,* since it is the *basis* for establishing the stock, markdown and purchase figures. It is the one that requires the greatest judgment since its accuracy depends on careful research and analysis.

STEP 1: *Forecast* carefully future *total dollar sales volume* for the *entire* period.

a. *Review* and *analyze past sales* performance for the *same time period*.
b. *Consider* factors that may cause a *change* in sales. Such factors include:

- Current sales trends
- Previous rate of growth patterns
- Economic conditions
- Local business conditions
- Fashion factors
- Influencing conditions within and from outside the store or department.

c. *Establish,* for the season, a percent of estimated sales change once the *past* sales performance and current conditions causing sales changes have been reviewed and analyzed. Then the *total dollar sales volume* for the entire period can be calculated. The common procedure is as follows:

1. Calculating a total planned seasonal sales figure when last year's sales and the planned percent of increase are known.

CONCEPT: Seasonal Planned Sales = Last Year (L.Y.) sales × planned increase percent
= Dollar Increase
= L.Y. Sales + Dollar Increase

PROBLEM: If last year's seasonal sales are $1,834,900 and there was a planned 9% sales increase, what are the planned seasonal sales for this year?

SOLUTION: Seasonal Planned Sales = $1,834,900 L.Y. Sales
× .09 Sales Increase
= $1,834,900 L.Y. Sales
+ $165,141 Sales Increase
SEASONAL PLANNED SALES = $2,000,041*

---

*On the actual plan the seasonal planned sales would be projected at $2,000,000.

2. Calculating percent of sales increase or decrease when last year's (L.Y.) actual sales and this year's (T.Y.) planned sales are known.

CONCEPT: Percent Sales Increase or Decrease = T.Y. Planned Sales
− L.Y. Actual Sales
= Sales Increase

PROBLEM: If last year's actual sales were $1,834,900 and this year's planned sales are $2,000,000, what is the percent of sales increase?

SOLUTION: % Sales Increase = $2,000,000 Planned Sales
− $1,834,900 Actual L.Y. Sales
= $ 165,000 Sales Increase

$$= \frac{\$165,000 \text{ Sales Increase}}{\$1,834,900 \text{ L.Y. Sales}}$$

= .089

PERCENT SALES INCREASE = 9%

STEP 2: Set *individual* monthly sales goals.

a. *Consider* the department's *past experience* with respect to the normal *percentage distribution* of sales for the planning period.
b. *Compare* the monthly percentage distribution with industry performance.
c. *Adjust* monthly sales figures because of shifting dates of certain holidays, special promotions planned, etc.

2. Planning Stocks

Since the merchandising policies of retail stores differ, there is no appropriate formula in developing the *variety* of a stock assortment. However, the planning phase of stock *investment* is accomplished through the dollar plan. In the planning and control of *dollar* stocks *all* merchandisers' objectives are to:

- Maintain *adequate* (reasonably complete from a customer's viewpoint) assortments.
- Regulate the dollar investment of stocks in relation to sales in order to obtain a satisfactory *balance* between these two factors.

After planned monthly sales are established, the amounts of dollar stock that is required on hand at the beginning of each month (B.O.M. stocks) and/or the end of each month (E.O.M. stocks) must be determined. The E.O.M. stock for a particular month is the same as the B.O.M. stock for the following month; for example, if $230,000 is the E.O.M. stock for February, it is the B.O.M. stock for March.

There are variations in the method of calculating individual monthly stock figures. Before discussing these possible techniques we must turn our attention to TURNOVER which is the degree of balance between sales and stocks. The rate of stock turnover measures the velocity with which merchandise moves into and out of a department or store. Turnover (rate of stock turnover) is a merchandising figure. It indicates the number of times that an average stock has been sold and replaced durng a given period. It is a figure which shows the *number of times* goods have been turned into money, and money turned back into goods. For convenience of comparison, it is usually expressed as an annual or semiannual figure. Despite the fact that turnover is a *resultant* figure, it *can* be planned and controlled.

Determining the turnover figure.
Every retailer should understand the importance of turnover in order to make better use of his capital investment, to control inventories, and ultimately, to realize optimum profits. It acts as an index to merchandising efficiently. Successful stock planning does not begin with turnover. Successful stock planning *results* in achieving the desired *rate of stock turnover*. This term indicates the number of times that an *average stock* is sold for a given period of time, which, unless otherwise stated, refers to a period of *one* year. However, it may be computed on a weekly, monthly, or seasonal basis. The actual *number of stock turns* varies with the *type of merchandise* and *price*. Generally speaking, lower price ranges turn more rapidly than higher ranges; apparel and accessories turn more rapidly than home furnishings. *Typical* average turnover figures for a particular type of goods have their greatest importance as a method of comparison. The following *average* rate of turnover figures show the range that may occur:

Misses Dresses	4.5
Men's Clothing	2.5
Sleepwear and Robes	4.5
Children's Footwear	2.2
Linens & Domestics	2.2
Hats	3.8

What is the importance of turnover to a merchandising operation?

- Stimulates sales by presenting fresh merchandise to the customer
- Reduces markdowns by keeping the flow of new goods constant, thereby curbing the accumulation of large amounts of older stock
- Lowers cost of goods sold because the "open to buy" position permits the buyer to take advantage of special prices and offerings
- Decreases interest, merchandise taxes and other operating expenses as a percentage of net sales.

The stock turnover rate can be calculated on either a unit or dollar basis. We shall confine our discussion to the dollar basis.

a. **Calculating Turnover When Average Stock and Sales for the Period Are Known***

Stock turn using dollar figures can be determined on either a cost or retail basis. In stores that use the retail method of inventory, the rate of stock turn is generally determined on the *retail* basis. Essential for accuracy is that *both sales and inventory* be upon the *same* basis.

CONCEPT: $\text{Turnover} = \dfrac{\text{Net Sales for period}}{\text{Average stock for same period}}$

PROBLEM: For the year, the infants' department had net sales of $2,000,000. The average stock during this period was $500,000. What was the rate of stock turn?

SOLUTION: $\text{Turnover for the period} = \dfrac{\$2,000,000 \text{ Net sales}}{\$500,000 \text{ Average stock}}$

TURNOVER = 4

b. **Calculating Average Stock When Planned Sales and Turnover Are Known**

CONCEPT: $\text{Average Stock} = \dfrac{\text{Planned sales for period}}{\text{Turnover rate}}$

PROBLEM: A hosiery department planned sales of $2,000,000 and wanted to achieve a stock turn of 4. What should be the average stock carried for the period under consideration?

SOLUTION: $\text{Average Stock for period} = \dfrac{\$2,000,000 \text{ Planned sales}}{4 \text{ Turnover rate}}$

AVERAGE STOCK = $500,000

c. **Calculating Average Stock When Monthly Inventories Are Known**

Since the determination of the average inventory directly affects the rate of stock turn, there is a need for a common method among stores to determine the average stock amounts so that the comparison of stock turns can be meaningful. *Under the retail method of inventory,* an AVERAGE STOCK is the sum of the retail inventories at the beginning of each year, season, month or week, added to the ending inventory and divided by the number of inventories used. This is the most *accurate* and commonly used method since a monthly book inventory figure is available. For example, to obtain an average stock for a year, the 12 stock inventories at the *beginning of each month* are added to the *ending* inventory and the total sum is divided by 13. If the stock turnover rate is computed for a shorter period than one year, the same principle is applied; e.g., for determining a six-month turnover rate, add the *seven* stock-on-hand figures and divide by 7. The turnover rate computed for a period, less than a year, can be converted to an equivalent annual rate.

---

*The same method can be used to calculate either a monthly or yearly turnover figure.

CONCEPT: Average Stock = $\dfrac{\text{Sum of beginning inventories} + \text{Ending inventory for given period}}{\text{Number of Inventories}}$

PROBLEM: Find the average stock and the turnover for this period.

Sales		B.O.M. Stocks	
January	$10,000	Jan. 1	$13,000
February	8,000	Feb. 1	12,000
March	14,000	Mar. 1	17,000
April	16,000	Apr. 1	19,000
May	12,000	May 1	15,000
June	14,000	June 1	18,000
July	10,000	July 1	14,000
August	6,000	Aug. 1	10,000
September	12,000	Sept. 1	16,000
October	11,000	Oct. 1	15,000
November	12,000	Nov. 1	15,000
December	15,000	Dec. 1	18,000
		Dec. 31	($13,000 is ending inventory)

SOLUTION:
Sum of 12 B.O.M. Stocks = $182,000
E.O.M. Stock (Plus) = + 13,000
= $195,000

Average Stock = $\dfrac{\$195{,}000 \text{ (Sum of 13 figures)}}{13 \text{ (Number of inventories)}}$

AVERAGE STOCK
for one year = $15,000

To now figure the turnover rate, having calculated an average stock figure, the formula of net sales divided by the average stock is applied; e.g.,

Turnover = $\dfrac{\$140{,}000 \text{ (Sum of 12 monthly sales figures)}}{\$15{,}000 \text{ (Average stock for the period)}}$

TURNOVER = 9.3

The same method is used to calculate an average stock for a shorter period.

The following problem applies the formulas for average inventory and turnover. It illustrates *determining the average stock for a shorter period than one year*, and shows how to *convert the turnover to an annual rate*.

EXAMPLE:

	Sales	Stock on Hand (*Book Inventory*)
Feb. 1	$ 20,000	$ 50,000
Mar. 1	27,500	60,000
Apr. 1	35,000	75,000
May 1	32,500	70,000
May 31		60,000
Total Sales	$115,000	$315,000
		Sum of Inventories

$$\text{Average stock} = \frac{\$315,000 \text{ Sum of inventories}}{5 \text{ No. of inventories}}$$

Average stock = $63,000

$$\text{Stock turn rate} = \frac{\$115,000 \text{ Net sales}}{\$63,000 \text{ Average stock}}$$

$$= 1.83 \text{ for 4 months or } \tfrac{1}{3} \text{ year}$$

Annual Rate = 1.83 × 3

ANNUAL TURN-OVER RATE = 5.49

To plan stocks for a season, from the *standpoint of stock turnover,* involves apportioning merchandise so that the *average* stock is related to the sales for the entire period. This approach *does not* offer a basis for planning a *specific* amount of stock to be on hand to achieve a planned sales figure.

Methods of Stock Planning.
It is common to plan monthly stock figures for the beginning of the period by a STOCK-SALES RATIO method.

1. *Setting individual first of month stock figures by Stock-Sales Ratio Method.*
   After planned monthly sales figures are established, the amount of dollar stock that is required on hand at the beginning of each month (B.O.M. STOCKS) and the end of each month (E.O.M. STOCKS) must be determined. This relationship is referred to as a STOCK-SALES RATIO. The B.O.M. stock-sales ratio is more commonly used in balancing planned *monthly* stocks to the planned *monthly* sales. Standard stock-sales ratios in departments can be established by evaluating one's own *past performance* that has proven to provide the proper relationship. In addition, researched guidelines of data showing *typical monthly* stock-sales ratios are available, and this can be used as a source of information in planning monthly stock proportions. Since monthly stock-sales proportions vary, it is necessary to establish the proper ratio for an *individual* month.

FIGURE 17. TYPICAL MONTHLY STOCK-SALES RATIO BY DEPARTMENTS

	Jan.	Feb.	Mar.	Apr.	May	June	July	Aug.	Sept.	Oct.	Nov.	Dec.
Girls' Clothing	6.8	6.4	3.7	5.4	6.2	7.2	5.8	4.4	5.2	5.0	4.5	3.2
Millinery	2.6	13.1	2.2	3.3	3.7	3.2	2.8	3.0	3.4	3.8	3.2	1.9
Lingerie	4.7	4.6	5.5	5.2	3.8	4.3	4.3	3.9	5.0	4.7	4.0	1.8
Dressy Coats	2.1	2.6	2.3	2.4	3.8	4.7	3.9	4.5	5.0	3.3	2.7	1.9

FIGURE 18. STOCK SALES RATIOS BY STORE VOLUME

Department Stores Stock Sales Ratios

Store Volume	Feb	Mar	Apr	May	Jun	Jul	Aug	Sept	Oct	Nov	Dec	Jan
$1-5 Million	5.12	4.60	4.32	4.39	4.29	4.64	4.00	4.57	4.88	4.28	2.65	5.08
$5-10 Million	6.31	5.09	5.62	5.65	5.68	5.91	5.40	5.12	5.61	5.14	2.87	6.06
$10-20 Million	5.67	4.91	5.82	5.36	4.95	5.18	4.51	4.44	5.11	4.80	2.58	5.32
$20-50 Million	6.21	4.76	4.53	5.17	6.43	6.26	4.61	4.84	4.56	4.33	2.65	4.14
$50-$100 Million	4.50	4.97	4.92	4.87	4.37	5.87	5.51	4.94	5.02	4.73	2.45	4.95
Over $100 Million	6.72	4.48	5.55	5.24	4.55	4.57	5.12	4.36	5.79	4.37	2.88	6.48

a. Calculating Stock-Sales Ratio When Retail Stock and Sales for a Given Period Are Known

CONCEPT: Stock-Sales Ratio $= \dfrac{\text{Retail stock at given time in the period}}{\text{Sales for the period}}$

PROBLEM: The boys' wear department on Feb. 1 had a retail stock of $120,000. The sales planned for this month were $20,000. Find the stock-sales ratio for the month of February.

SOLUTION: Stock-Sales Ratio $= \dfrac{\$120{,}000 \text{ B.O.M. stock}}{\$20{,}000 \text{ Feb. sales}}$

STOCK-SALES RATIO = 6

b. Calculating B.O.M. Stock When Planned Sales and Stock-Sales Ratio Are Known

CONCEPT: B.O.M. Stock = Planned monthly sales × Stock-sales ratio

PROBLEM: The yard goods department planned sales of $40,000 for the month of July. The departmental past experience showed an 8.2 stock-sales ratio was successful. What should be the planned B.O.M. stock for July?

SOLUTION: B.O.M. July Stock = $\begin{array}{r}\$\ 40{,}000 \text{ Planned July sales} \\ \times\ \ \ 8.2 \text{ Stock-sales ratio} \\ \hline \end{array}$

B.O.M. STOCK = $328,000

2. *Setting stock figures by Weeks Supply Method.*

This method of stock planning is best used in a department that primarily carries staple merchandise and/or has a relatively stable sales volume. Since the stock size is in direct relation to the planned weekly sales, it can result in an excessive stock condition at the peak selling periods or in dangerously low stocks during the slower months.

This technique plans inventory size on a weekly basis. The amount of stock set equals a calculated number of weeks supply. The number of weeks supply that is to be "on hand" depends on the *planned turnover* figure to be achieved and is used to guide or *set* the number of weeks inventory supply.

a. **Calculating the Number of Weeks Supply**

    CONCEPT: The Number of Weeks Supply = Weeks ÷ Desired turnover

    PROBLEM: Department #32 has a planned stock turnover of 4.0 for the 6-month period. Determine the number of weeks supply needed to achieve the desired turnover.

    SOLUTION: The Number of Weeks Supply $= \dfrac{26 \text{ weeks (6 month)}}{4.0 \text{ turnover}}$

    THE NUMBER OF WEEKS SUPPLY = 6.5

b. **Finding Planned Stock, Given Turnover and Weekly Rate of Sales**

    CONCEPT: Planned Stock = Average weekly sales × the number of weeks supply

    PROBLEM: A department has an average weekly sales rate of $9,800 and a planned turnover of 4.0 for the 6-month period. Calculate the amount of stock to be carried.

    SOLUTION: Step 1. Find the Number of Weeks Supply given turnover and supply period.

    The Number of Weeks Supply $= \dfrac{26 \text{ weeks (6 month)}}{4.0 \text{ turnover}}$

    THE NUMBER OF WEEKS SUPPLY = 6.5

    Step 2. Find Planned Stock given average weekly sales and number of weeks supply.

    Planned Stock = $9,800 Average Weekly Sales × 6.5 Number of Weeks Supply

    PLANNED STOCK = $63,700

PRACTICE PROBLEMS

1. Sales for last year (season) were $855,000 and the merchandise manager planned for a sales increase, this year, of 8%. What is the estimated planned sales figure for this year?

2. Actual sales for last year were $855,000 and this years' planned sales are $923,400, calculate the percentage of sales increase this year over last year.

3. A handbag department plans a stock turn at 6.0 for a twelve-month period. What figure would represent the number of *weeks supply* needed to achieve the desired turnover?

4. A glove department has an average weekly sales figure of $14,500 and a planned turnover of 3.0 for the six-month period. Calculate the amount of stock to be carried under the conditions outlined.

5. What is the planned stock-sales ratio in the handbag department when beginning of the month stock is planned at $19,000 and planned sales are $9,100?

6. Planned sales in the costume jewelry department for April are $130,000 and the planned stock-sales ratio is 2.4. What should be the stock on April 1?

7. In the lingerie department, it was decided for the month of February that a stock-sales ratio of 2.5 would be correct. If the sales for February were planned at $12,000, how much stock should be carried on February 1?

8. The glove department's stock at the beginning of March was $67,500. Sales for the month were $15,900. What was the stock-sales ratio for March?

9. What amount of average stock should be carried by a department with net sales for the year of $920,000 and a stock turn of 4?

10. What is the average stock of a department with annual sales of $1,350,000 and an annual stock turn of 4.5?

11. Calculate the yearly turnover:

Gross sales	$497,500
Customer returns	47,500
Inventory 8/1	85,000
Inventory 10/1	105,000
Inventory 12/1	250,000
Inventory 2/1	53,000
Inventory 4/1	90,000
Inventory 6/1	80,000
Inventory 8/1	76,000

12. For the year, a shoe department has net sales of $2,500,000. The average stock carried during this period was $1,000,000. What was the annual rate of stock turn?

13. Find the average stock from the following inventory figures:

B.O.M.	January	$62,000
B.O.M.	February	64,000
B.O.M.	March	70,000
B.O.M.	April	74,000
B.O.M.	May	88,000
B.O.M.	June	100,000
B.O.M.	July	120,000
B.O.M.	August	78,000
B.O.M.	September	78,000
B.O.M.	October	68,000
B.O.M.	November	64,000
B.O.M.	December	60,000
E.O.M.	December	62,000

14. Departmental *gross* sales for the year were $220,000 with customer returns of 10%. During the year these inventories were taken:

Date	Inventory Value (Retail)
January 1	$37,000
April 1	36,500
July 1	41,500
October 1	46,500
Jan. 1 of following year	38,500

    Find:

    a. average stock for the year.
    b. annual rate of turn.

15. The sales for October were $8,000; the stock October 1 at retail value was $24,000; the stock October 31 was $28,000. What was the stock turn for the month?

16. The sales in the children's department for the year amounted to $416,000. The stock at the beginning of the year was $120,000 at retail, and for the end of the year, the retail stock figure was $140,000. What was the stock turn for this period?

3. Planning Markdowns

In dollar planning it is important to include markdowns because they *reduce the total value of the stock available for sales*. The careful *planning of markdowns helps reduce the amount taken* and this is a means of increasing the net profit figures. The amount of planned markdowns to be taken is expressed both in *dollars* and as a *percentage of planned sales*. Since the *dollar* markdowns taken vary greatly, the *percentage* data is more significant for *comparison* of past and present performance. The percentage of markdowns taken also varies with different lines of merchandise, different months and different seasons. The planned markdown figure is usually based on a *normal* amount determined from past experience. Typical markdown percentages are available for industry comparison, as illustrated below.

FIGURE 19. TYPICAL MARKDOWN PERCENTAGES

ANNUAL MARKDOWN % (expressed as a % of net sales)			
Women's Footwear	14.5%	Boys' Clothing	10.0%
All Dresses	19.6%	Small Appliances	5.1%
Infants & Toddlers	10.4%	Cosmetics & Toiletries	1.5%

STEP 1: Set the *total markdown amount* (stated as a *percentage of total season's sales*) for the entire period.

    a. *Review* and *analyze* past markdown performance for the same period, for the entire period under consideration.
    b. *Consider factors* that may affect a *change* in markdowns.

STEP 2: *Convert* the planned markdown *percentage* of sales to a *total dollar figure for the season*.

STEP 3: *Apportion* total *dollar* planned markdowns by *month*. (Distribution of monthly markdown goals does *not* necessarily mean that markdowns and sales will be in the same proportion during each of the months of the season.)

    EXAMPLE: *Planning Markdowns*
    Last year, the net sales for the season in the glove department were $100,000. The total amount of markdowns taken during the entire period totaled $5,000. The buyer, upon reviewing his past performance, in preparation of planning his markdowns for the same period this year, decided the $5,000 markdown figure previously taken was normal and compared favorably with standard markdown *percentages* established for his type of merchandise. Therefore, he *converted last year's dollar markdown amount* to a percentage:

$$\frac{\$5,000 \text{ Last Year's Markdown}}{\$100,000 \text{ Last Year's Net Sales}} = 5\% \text{ Markdowns}$$

The total planned sales figure established by the buyer for the season under consideration was set at $110,000. Since he wanted to repeat the *percentage* of markdowns for the forthcoming season, he *determined the dollar amount of markdowns* to be taken by:

$110,000 Planned sales × 5% Planned markdowns
= $5,500 Planned total markdown for the season

$5,500 would then be *apportioned to the individual months* of the period.

4. Planning Markup on Purchases

Markup planning and calculations are treated in depth in Unit Three. It is sufficient now to add that after the initial markup has been carefully planned, the buyer will have to constantly manipulate the actual markup to date with the markup on additional purchases for the season in order to obtain the *planned* seasonal markup percentage.

In order to "protect" profitability, the gross profit figure, including an estimated shortage amount can now easily be calculated in the following manner.

Given:

Dollar Sales (from plan)		$2,000,000
Dollar Markdown (from plan)	300,000	
Anticipated Dollar Shortage (shortage % × total planned dollar sales)	40,000	
Planned MU% on Stock + Purchases	49.07%	
Cost or Complement % on Planned Stock + Purchases	50.93%	

Cost of Planned Sales:

Pl. MD   = $ 300,000 × .5093 =   152,790
Pl. Shortage = $ 40,000 × .5093 =   20,372
Pl. Sales   = $2,000,000 × .5093 =   1,018,600
                          total $1,191,762

                                              −1,191,762
PLANNED $ GROSS PROFIT = $ 808,238

PLANNED GROSS PROFIT % = $ 808,238
                          2,000,000
                        = 40.2%

5. Planned Purchases

An objective of planning is to assist the buyer in proper timing and in purchasing amounts of goods. Therefore, once the planned sales, stocks and markdowns have been determined, the amount of monthly purchases is automatically calculated by a formula. The term PLANNED PURCHASES refers to the dollar amount of merchandise that can be *brought into stock during a given period*. Purchases are generally pre-planned for *each* month at retail value and then converted, by formula, to a cost figure by applying the planned markup.

a. Calculating Planned Monthly Purchases (Retail)

CONCEPT: Planned Monthly Purchase = Planned E.O.M. stock
  + Planned sales for month
  + Planned markdowns for month
  = Total merchandise requirements
  − Planned B.O.M. stock
  = Planned purchase amount

PROBLEM: For the lingerie department, calculate from the following planned figures the planned purchase amount for June:

Planned stock June 1	$ 38,000
Planned sales for June	100,000
Planned markdowns for June	5,000
Planned stock for July 1	40,000

SOLUTION:

Planned June sales	=	$100,000
Planned E.O.M. stock	=	40,000
Planned June markdowns	=	5,000
Total merchandise requirements	=	$145,000
(minus) Planned B.O.M. stock	=	− 38,000
PLANNED PURCHASES	=	$107,000

b. Converting Retail Planned Purchases at Cost

CONCEPT: Pl. Purch. at Cost = Pl. purch. (retail) × (100% − Pl. MU%)

PROBLEM: The planned retail purchases for February were $103,000, and the planned MU% was 41.5%. Calculate the planned purchase amount at cost.

SOLUTION: Planned purchases = $103,000 Planned retail purchases ×
at cost (100% − 41.5% Planned MU%)
= $103,000 × 58.5%

PLANNED PURCHASES AT COST = $60,255

c. Adjusting the Planned Purchases

During the season, as the merchandising activities are performed, the *actual* results are checked against the planned figures. This reveals the need, perhaps, to adjust the original planned figures for either a month or the balance of the season, in light of what has happened thus far or current circumstances. For example, if sales and/or markdowns are actually larger than planned, purchases must be greater than planned to achieve the level of stock planned. If these factors are actually less than planned, it means a downward revision of purchases. The following illustrates the variation between planned figures and actual results:

FIGURE 20. PURCHASE PLANNING

Planned

	$20,000	Planned Sales
Planned purchases for October	+42,000	Planned E.O.M. Stock
based on *planned* figures	+ 500	Planned Markdowns
	$62,500	Total Merchandise Requirements
	−40,000	Planned B.O.M. Stock
PLANNED PURCHASES =	$22,500	

Revised

	$22,000	Revised Sales Plan
Planned purchases for October	+42,000	Planned E.O.M. Stock
based on *revised* figures	+ 500	Revised Markdowns
	$64,500	Total Merchandise Requirements
	−40,000	Revised B.O.M. Stock
ADJUSTED PLANNED PURCHASES =	$24,500	

NOTES

PRACTICE PROBLEMS

1. Calculate the gross profit, as a dollar figure, given the following situation:

Dollar sales (given)	$900,000
Dollar markdowns (given)	135,000
Dollar shortage (estimated)	18,000
Percent planned markup on stock & purchases	48.5%
Reciprocal percent planned markup	51.5%

2. Find the planned June purchases if:

Planned June sales	$ 72,000
Planned June markdowns	3,000
Planned stock June 1	150,600
Planned stock July 1	155,600

3. Calculate the planned July purchases at cost:

    Planned July sales $175,000
    Planned July markdowns   20,000
    Planned stock July 1   250,000
    Planned stock July 31   125,000
    Planned markup   42%

4. Note the following figures:

    Planned September sales $18,000
    Planned September markdowns   800
    Planned stock September 1   49,200
    Planned stock October 1   50,400
    Planned markup   41½%

    a. Determine the planned September purchases at retail.
    b. Determine the planned September purchases at cost.
    c. What is the turnover for September?

5. The hosiery department has an initial markup of 54%. The sales planned for September are $10,000 and for October $12,000. The desired B.O.M. stock-sales ratio for September is 2 and for October is 1.5. The planned markdowns are $600.

   a. What are the planned September purchases at retail?
   b. What are the planned September purchases at cost?

6. From the following figures determine the:

   a. Original planned purchases.
   b. Adjusted planned purchases.

Planned stock November 1	$147,000
Planned stock December 1	110,000
Planned November markdowns	2,000
Planned November sales	63,000
Actual stock November 1	140,000
Actual November sales	61,000

II. OPEN-TO-BUY CONTROL

Merchandise *control* results from *effective* use of data available through the dollar planning procedure. A buyer purchases merchandise guided by the timing and quantity goals established in his six-month seasonal dollar plan. To provide a *tighter control* for the amount of merchandise received in a specific period and to achieve the sales and stock plans, he refers to a merchandising figure called OPEN-TO-BUY. This term, abbreviated OTB, denotes the amount of *unspent* (order limit) money that is available for purchasing merchandise *to be delivered* during a given period. It is usually figured on a monthly basis and indicates that the buyer has *not yet spent* all of his planned purchases for the period in question. It represents the *difference* between the planned purchases for a period and the merchandise orders already placed for that period. Unfilled orders, known as open orders or "on order," should be charged to those months during which delivery is expected so that the buyer is able to *control* and *time* his buying activities to correlate with his selling activities. The purpose of control is to identify deviations between actual results and planned goals and to take corrective measures when needed.

The planned purchase figure for a particular month indicates the sum with which to purchase goods *during* the month, but does not distribute the money *throughout* the month. Experienced buyers attempt to distribute purchases *over the entire month* for the following reasons:

- To reorder fast selling goods
- To fill-in stocks to offer complete stocks
- To have the competitive advantage to buy available special purchases and new and interesting items
- To test offerings of new resources

Current information which shows developments as they happen helps assure that the planned factors will proceed according to plan. Therefore, in large stores it is common that the controller's office report periodically. The typical report includes the following information:

- Sales
  - Planned for the month
  - This month to date
  - Adjusted plan for month
- Stocks
  - First of month
  - Receipts to date (additions)
  - On hand today
  - Planned E.O.M. stock
  - Adjusted E.O.M. stock
- Purchases
  - Planned for month
  - Adjusted plan for month
  - Plan for next month
- Outstanding Orders
  - For delivery by month
- Markdowns
  - Season to date at B.O.M. in dollars
  - Season to date at B.O.M. in % to sales
  - Month to date
- Open-to-Buy
  - Balance for current month
- Cumulative Markup
  - Plan for month
  - Actual to date

A. Calculating Open-to-Buy at the Beginning of a Month

CONCEPT: OTB = Planned purchases for the month −
Outstanding orders to be delivered that month

PROBLEM: A buyer has planned January sales of $60,000 with an opening January stock planned at $50,000 and a closing stock of $30,000. The markdowns were planned at $500. If he has already placed orders amounting to $10,000 at retail for January delivery, what is his January open-to-buy?

SOLUTION:

Jan. sales	=	$60,000
(plus) Jan. E.O.M. stock	=	30,000
(plus) Jan. markdowns	=	500
	=	$90,500
(minus) Jan. B.O.M. stock	=	−50,000
Jan. planned purchases	=	$40,500
(minus) Jan. on order	=	−10,000
Jan. OTB	=	$30,500

B. Calculating Open-to-Buy During the Month

If the buyer wishes to calculate the OTB figure at a certain time *during* the period, he may base his calculations either on the *predetermined planned purchases* or determine the open-to-buy figure for the balance of the period by *figuring back from the planned closing stock*. Illustrative problems follow.

1. OTB for Balance of Month Based on Predetermined Planned Purchases

CONCEPT: OTB for balance of month = Planned purchases for month −
Merchandise received to date −
On order

PROBLEM: The merchandise plan shows that the planned purchases for September amount to $17,000. The store's records show that from September 1 to September 15 the department received $8,300 worth of new goods and there is an order of $700 for delivery in September. What is the open-to-buy for the balance of the month?

SOLUTION:

Sept. planned purchases	=	$17,000
(minus) Merchandise received	=	−8,300
(minus) On order	=	− 700
SEPTEMBER OTB BALANCE	=	$ 8,000

2. OTB for Balance of Month Based on Planned Closing Stock

CONCEPT: OTB for Balance of Month
= Planned sales for balance of month
+ Planned markdowns for balance of month
+ Planned E.O.M. stock
= Total merchandise requirements
− Actual stock on hand
− On order
= OTB for balance of the month

PROBLEM: On September 15, a department has a stock of $26,000 and merchandise on order amounting to $700. The planned sales for the balance of September are $8,000 and the planned markdowns for the balance of the month are $500. The stock planned for September 30 is $31,800. What is the OTB for the balance of the month?

SOLUTION:

Planned sales for balance of month	= $ 8,000
(plus) Planned markdowns for balance of month	= 500
(plus) Planned E.O.M. stock	= 31,800
Total merchandise requirements	= $ 40,300
(minus) Actual stock on hand	= −26,000
(minus) On order	= − 700
SEPTEMBER OTB BALANCE	= $ 13,600

NOTES

PRACTICE PROBLEMS

1. What is the open-to-buy for a department with planned purchases of $71,500 and outstanding orders of $74,000?

2. The actual stock on April 1 is $116,000 with "on order" in April amounting to $18,000. Sales are planned at $75,000, with markdowns estimated to be 3.5%; the stock on April 30 is planned at $112,000. What is the OTB for this month?

3. Find the balance of the open-to-buy for March when March 13 stock on hand is $16,300 and planned sales for the balance of the month are $9,000. Merchandise on order amounts to $3,000 and the planned April 1 stock is $10,000.

4. The May portion of a 6-month plan for a shop is as follows:

    Planned May sales $37,500
    Planned May markdowns   10%
    Planned May B.O.M. stock   66,000
    Planned June B.O.M. stock   59,000
    Planned markup   49%

    a. What are the planned May purchases at retail?
    b. On May 1, the buyer is notified that $8,000 worth of goods (retail value) is on order. What is the open-to-buy at cost for May?

5. Find the balance of OTB for December when the stock on hand December 10 is $265,000 and the planned sales for the balance of the month are $171,000. Planned markdowns amount to $11,000 and planned December 31 inventory is $150,000. Outstanding orders total $71,500.

PRACTICE PROBLEMS FOR REVIEW OF UNIT FIVE

1. A housewares department in a major West Coast retail store operates on a planned stock turn figure of 4.0 for the period August 1 to February 1. How would the number of *weeks supply* be expressed?

2. The annual turnover figure for an apparel department is projected at 5.0. Express the stated relationship in terms of *weeks supply*.

3. Average weekly sales in an automotive supply department of a major national chain is stated at $3,400,000. Turnover in this classification of merchandise is 4.0 annually. Calculate the stock figure which it would be appropriate to carry under these conditions.

4. Turnover is planned at 2.5 for the six month period February 1 through July 31. Average weekly sales for that period are $75,000. What average stock should be carried in this situation?

5. A major department store chain, after careful analysis of economic projections distributed by the U.S. Department of Commerce, set a figure of 7.5% as a realistic increase for this year's business volume over last. Last year, the corporate volume was $3,700,000,000. What figure is projected for this year?

6. A Dallas-based specialty chain had sales of $196,000,000 last year. It plans $216,000,000 for the coming year. What percentage increase is it projecting?

7. March figures for a shoe department are as follows:

Planned sales	$510,000
Planned markdowns	6,000
Planned March 1 stock	906,000
Planned April 1 stock	630,000
Outstanding March orders	126,000
Planned markup	52%

a. What were the planned March purchases at retail?
b. What is the March open-to-buy at cost?

8. Find planned June purchases if:

Planned sales	$22,000
B.O.M. stock June	44,000
B.O.M. stock July	40,000
Planned June markdown	1,000

a. Find OTB at retail, if "on order" for June delivery is $16,000 at retail.
b. Find OTB at cost, if planned markup is 56%.

9. Note the following figures:

       Planned sales $85,000
       Planned markdowns   1,000
       Planned B.O.M. stock   151,000
       Planned E.O.M. stock   105,000
       Merchandise on order   21,000
       Planned markup   51%

   a. Determine the original planned purchases at cost.
   b. Determine the OTB at retail.

10. Find the planned June purchases; the June OTB; the June turnover.

       Planned sales $22,000
       B.O.M. stock June   44,000
       B.O.M. stock July   40,000
       "On order" for June delivery   16,000
       Planned June markdowns   1,000

11. What is the OTB for a department with planned purchases of $56,000 and an "on order" of $19,000?

12. Net sales last year were $185,220. Inventories were:

Dates	Stock on Hand
12/30/77	$ 36,000
3/31/78	42,000
6/30/78	41,000
1/3/79	49,000
	$168,000

    What was the stock turn?

13. The stock-sales ratio in the shirt department has been set at 3.4 for June. Sales are planned at $34,500. What is the B.O.M. stock for June?

14. Determine the B.O.M. stock-sales ratio when the planned sales for April are $56,000 and the retail value of stock on hand for April 1 is $84,000.

15. Find planned purchases for May: a. at retail; b. at cost.

Planned sales for May	$36,000
Planned markdowns	1,500
Planned stock May 1	75,300
Planned stock June 1	77,800
Planned markup	50%

16. The sales for August were $27,000. The stock on August 1 was $81,000 and the stock on August 31 was $69,000. What was the stock turn for the month?

17. Find planned purchases for October:

Planned sales	$46,000
Planned markdowns	6,500
Planned September E.O.M. stock	68,000
Planned October E.O.M. stock	54,000
Planned markup	48%

    a. at retail
    b. at cost
    c. On October 1, the buyer calculates that $16,000 worth of merchandise at retail is on order. What is the OTB at cost for October?

18. A boutique shop had net sales of $760,000 for a six-month period ending August 31. The monthly retail inventories were:

Dates	Stock on Hand
Feb. 1	$ 78,000
March 1	130,000
April 1	217,600
May 1	306,600
June 1	197,840
July 1	132,880
July 31	118,700
	$1,181,620

    a. Find the turnover for the six-month period.
    b. Calculate the stock-sales ratio for May, if the sales for the month were $146,000.

19. A hosiery buyer took a physical inventory of stock every three months. The stock counts showed the following inventory valuations:

Dates	Stock on Hand
January 3	$16,390
April 2	18,412
July 1	14,473
October 2	19,670
December 31	15,880
	$84,825

What was the department's average stock for the elapsed year?

20. Determine the turnover for a department with the following figures:

Month	Sales	B.O.M. Stocks
February	$30,000	$ 75,000
March	45,000	90,000
April	60,000	120,000
May	70,000	135,000
June	75,000	90,000
July	45,000	60,000
August		65,000

210

21. Find the balance of November open-to-buy for a dress department with these plans:

Planned sales for balance of November	$18,000
Planned markdowns for balance of November	600
Planned stock for December 1	20,000
Merchandise on order for November delivery	6,000
Stock on hand	32,600

22. Planned sales for the 6-month period February through July in a dress department were $250,000. The monthly inventories at retail for this period were:

Dates	Stock on Hand
February 1	$ 90,000
March 1	87,000
April 1	92,000
May 1	90,000
June 1	84,000
July 1	79,000
July 31	62,000
	$584,000

a. What is the planned average stock for the period?
b. What is the planned annual turnover based on this period?
c. If planned sales in April were $23,000, what is the stock-sales ratio for April?

23.

	B.O.M. Stocks	Net Sales
January	$ 50,000	$ 15,000
February	46,000	18,000
March	46,000	20,000
April	46,000	14,000
May	40,000	12,000
June	40,000	16,000
July	45,000	14,000
August	45,000	14,000
September	50,000	18,000
October	60,000	18,000
November	80,000	38,000
December	44,000	16,000
January (following year)	46,000	$213,000
	$638,000	

Find:

a. Yearly average stock.
b. Turnover for year.
c. Turnover for September.
d. Stock-sales ratio for June.

24. The Statistical Division provides a buyer with the following computerized information. Determine balance-of-the-month OTB.

Planned sales for balance of month	$162,000
Planned markdowns for balance of month	4,000
Planned E.O.M. stock	200,000
Merchandise on order this month	64,000
Stock figure this date	214,000

*25. Describe how a buyer may use turnover and stock-sales ratio figures in planning a future departmental operation.

---

*For research and discussion.

213

*26. Are turnover and stock-sales ratio related? Explain.

*27. Does an increased turnover rate always mean that the department is functioning more and more effectively and profitably? Explain.

*For research and discussion.

*28. Is it merchandising "treason" to *plan* to be out of stock on a certain percent of the items you carry for a certain percent of the time? Why or why not? Discuss from the standpoint of the merchant and of the customer. Have certain very specialized retailers entered into this type of situation? Explain.

*29. Your merchandise manager calls you into her office and emphatically declares that your sales are far behind the plan to date. She tells you to draw up a plan of action and present it to her the next day. What remediation would you include in your report?

*For research and discussion.

NOTES

UNIT SIX

Periodic Merchandising and Operating Information

The preceding units of study have discussed the various factors which comprise a total merchandising operation. The elements involved in merchandising goods have been examined, revealing those elements which may contribute to, or detract from, the ultimate profit goals for a department, division, or the entire store. For the purpose of analysis, the *details* of the merchandising operation are vital. Periodic merchandising records furnish statistics which are the basis for merchandising planning and control, and make corrective action possible when necessary. The *analysis* and *interpretation* of the information supplied are aids for the buyer's decision-making. These reports are not a substitute for the buyer's own knowledge and experience, however.

Successful merchandisers know that effective merchandising requires *departmental* controls to insure a balanced stock, reflecting customer demands, and to minimize the dollar investment. The benefits of a better stock assortment and optimizing dollar investment are:

- greater sales results;
- fewer markdowns;
- increased gross margin;
- improved rate of stock turnover.

Department controls also permit management to judge the potential of each department and buyer to make a profit.

The control and supervision of the stock of merchandise has always been a soft spot in retailing. Retailers use two major merchandise control methods. One emphasizes the physical content of the stock; the other emphasizes the size or dollar value of the merchandise. This enables them to avoid being over- or under-stocked with "the right goods at the right time." In order to achieve balance between sales and stocks, data must be made available for analysis and interpreted to make the proper merchandising decisions.

The growth of multi-store operations mandated the need for prompt, accurate and complete facts upon which to make the necessary decisions. Since the 1960's, data-processing systems have provided retailers with this uninterrupted flow of information. In more recent years, the increased use of these systems by department stores as well as by mass merchandising chains has had a major impact on the management of merchandise inventories. Today, in retailing, the computer is a tool furnishing data which is helpful in identifying problems, and consequently, facilitating the decision-making process. Some of the benefits to retailers in using computers are:

- improved decision-making; great amounts of information can be processed in a short time; speed in recording and calculating transactions permit timely and accurate decisions;
- reduction of shortages through the reduction of data input errors at the point of sale;
- reduction of markdowns by providing earlier sales and merchandising information to buyers, thereby allowing corrective action on slow sellers;
- reduction of operational costs;
- improved selection of profitable resources;
- improved rate of turnover through fast action;
- protection of gross margin through fast action;
- improved inventory control.

The technical information associated with the operating procedures of the computer and with the various systems available will be avoided. Instead, emphasis will be on some of the information that relates to and affects the control of inventory, and ultimately, profit and loss.

Currently, retailers are benefiting from the countless applications of EDP (electronic data processing) in many areas. What is meant by *data processing*? It is a planned conversion of facts (as by computer) into usable or storable form to achieve a desired result. This information system is now commonly associated with the computer; therefore, it is labeled *electronic* data processing. In order for this system to be meaningful, the kinds of information and reports needed must be evaluated. The retailer must decide *which* reports are to be received and *how frequently*. Ideally, a computerized merchandising system should provide information about the physical stock which is in tandem with dollar control. Illustrations of records which furnish the desired information follow. The reports are divided into two major groupings. The first group shows typical applications for merchandise control; the second deals with financial or dollar control. Keep in mind that each retailer must decide what information and which reports will best serve his own situation.

I. REPORTS USED FOR MERCHANDISE CONTROL

The purpose of these reports is to aid the buyer in the balance and control of a stock which reflects customer demand. The following illustrations show factual information available concerning *merchandise classifications* and individual *style activity*. These records help keep track of inventory. The actual format as well as the amount of information provided may vary, but the function of these examples is the same.

A. Dollar Sales by Classification
This report provides weekly total sales information for each department, broken down by classification and store. Individual class totals, percentage contribution of class to total department sales, and cumulative contribution of class are listed. Dollar sales and its percentage are also given. This report may be available in weekly, monthly and seasonal forms. (See Figure 21.)

B. Classification-Price Line Report
This report contains all classifications and price lines of the department in both units and dollars. A complete history is given, and control is improved by knowledge of the net sales on hand, outstanding orders, receipts, transfers and markdowns as well as the stock-sales ratio for each group. The following reports (Figures 22 and 23) provide similar information, but are not identical.

C. Classification-Stock Status Report
The accuracy of this report (Figure 23) requires a check of Purchase Journals and Transfer Journals as well as Transit Items Reports. The OTB is constantly calculated and revised.

D. Monthly Sales and Stock Report
The dollar sales and units, on hand and on order, are summarized monthly to help balance merchandise inventory to sales demand. (See Figure 24.)

E. Fashion Report
This report enables the buyer to analyze the trend of each style and classification and to respond quickly to the selling history of each style as well as the sales/stock information. The following fashion reports (Figures 25 and 26) are similar and serve the same function, but the information furnished is not identical.

FIGURE 21. DOLLAR SALES BY CLASSIFICATION

DOLLAR SALES BY CLASSIFICATION
DEPARTMENT BY VOLUME REPORT FOR WEEK #09 ENDING 04/02 *** BUYER COPY ***

MC 362 SILVERWARE DEPT NUMBER 008

DEPT 008 CLASS	STORE 01	02	03	04	05	06	07	08	09	10	11	12	13	14	15	16	17	18	RT-22 RT-46	TOTAL
	10.6 22.6%	.7 1.4%	1.2 2.5%	.6 1.3%	3.3 7.1%	6.3 3.4%	3.1 6.6%	1.8 3.8%	3.4 7.2%	2.3 4.9%	1.9 3.9%	2.1 4.5%	2.0 4.2%	1.3 2.8%	1.4 3.0%	2.4 5.1%	.9 1.9%	1.8 3.8%		46,099
	DEPARTMENT TOTALS ***
15	STERLING FLATWARE 1633 15.4%	289 43.3%	399 13.9%		333 10.0%	2296 36.6%	1060 34.0%	628 35.4%	1137 33.4%	412 17.1%	493 26.6%	96 4.6%	1068 34.3%	99 7.5%	16 1.1%	1359 57.0%	13 1.4%	10 .6%		11,341 24% 24%
30	GUILD STAINLESS FLATWARE 1435 13.5%	54 8.1%	-135 11.5%	125 21.1%	699 21.0%	1156 18.4%	681 21.8%	462 26.1%	217 6.4%	567 24.4%	62 3.3%	649 30.9%	314 16.0%	495 37.4%	288 10.5%	499 20.9%	288 31.8%	522 29.4%		8,378 18% 42%
31	IMPORTED STAINLESS FLATWARE 5018 47.2%	-60 9.0%	164 13.9%		62 1.9%	177 2.8%	-20 .6%	-116 6.5%	145 4.3%	60 2.6%	73 3.9%	289 3.7%	-133 6.8%	164 12.4%	307 21.9%	74 3.1%	-16 1.8%	16 .9%		6,204 13% 55%
36	SILVERPLATED FLATWARE 996 9.4%		215 18.3%	170 28.7%	400 12.0%	734 11.7%	148 4.7%	136 7.7%	865 25.4%	152 6.5%	304 16.4%	299 14.2%	170 8.6%	380 28.7%	190 13.5%	130 5.5%		260 14.7%		5,549 12% 67%
20	SILVERPLATED HOLLOWARE 370 3.5%	120 19.5%	198 16.8%	120 20.3%	481 14.5%	468 7.5%	240 7.7%	244 13.8%	315 9.3%	373 16.1%	416 22.4%	270 12.8%	104 5.3%	324 24.5%	235 16.7%	114 4.8%	137 15.1%	356 20.1%		4,865 8% 85%
19	SILVERPLATED FOOD WARMERS, CHAFING DISHES, CASSEROLES 826 7.8%	159 23.8%	154 13.1%	63 10.6%	415 12.5%	384 6.1%	105 3.4%	150 8.5%	73 2.1%	328 14.1%	232 12.5%	106 5.0%	80 4.1%	176 12.5%	193 13.7%	37 1.6%	128 14.1%	88 5.0%		3,697 5% 90%
21	SILVERPLATED TEA & COFFEE SETS 272 2.6%	30 4.5%	60 5.1%	20 3.4%	144 4.3%	113 1.8%	365 11.7%	119 6.7%	352 10.3%	167 7.2%	105 5.7%	109 5.2%	123 6.3%	68 5.1%	-27 6.3%	123 5.1%	85 1.9%	142 9.4%		1,596 3% 93%
18	SILVERPLATED DRINKWARE 49 .5%	39 5.8%	28 2.4%	31 5.2%	88 2.6%	90 1.4%	186 6.0%	63 3.5%	173 5.1%	47 2.0%	134 7.2%	100 4.8%	111 5.6%	95 7.2%	157 11.2%	35 1.5%	42 4.6%	127 7.2%		1,472 3% 96%
11	STERLING HOLLOWARE & CANDLESTICKS 50 .5%	30 4.5%	63 5.4%	18 3.0%	435 13.1%	57 .9%	167 5.4%	75 4.2%	77 2.3%	138 5.8%	50 2.7%	68 3.2%	37 1.9%	46 3.5%	28 2.0%	13 .5%	55 6.1%	65 3.7%		2,370 6% 89%

219

FIGURE 22. CLASSIFICATION-PRICE LINE REPORT

CODE DESCRIPTION	STORE	NET SALES UNITS THIS WEEK ENDING 02/07	ONE WEEK AGO ENDING 01/31	2 WEEKS AGO ENDING 01/24	LAST 4 WEEKS ENDING 01/10	SEASON TO DATE 02/07	ON HAND UNITS	ON ORDER UNITS	MTD RECEIVING	MTD TRANS-FER	MTD MARKDOWN $	MTD MARKDOWN %	MTD NET SALES $	MTD NET SALES %	INVENTORY $	STOCK SALES RATIO	OPEN ORDER	INVENTORY ON ORDER	CODE NO
	14	2–				168	69												
	15		1	5	5	229	47												
CODE 96 TOTAL UNITS		2–	1	5	5	168													
TOTAL DOLLARS			8	14	31	1310	431												
		2–	106	177	381	17285	5683												
96 JEANS $15.01 – $20.00	01					48	51	120											96
	05					34	15	84											
	08					31	13	48											
	10					13	1	48											
	14					26	24	48											
	15					25	25	60											
CODE 96 TOTAL UNITS						177	129	408											
TOTAL DOLLARS						3142	2310	6528											
96 JEANS $20.01 – $29.00	01	4	1	1	5	5	5												96
	05	3		3	3	3	3–												
	08	2	1	2	3	5	3												
	10	4	1	3	5	5	5												
	14	2	1	6	3	3	3												
	15	1	3	1	4	4	4–												
CODE 96 TOTAL UNITS		16	7	15	23	23													
TOTAL DOLLARS		464	203	188	667	667	667–												
96 JEANS PRICE LINE-ALL	01	6	3	1	11	391	199	120					1	30	28	20	19	47	95
	05	3		3	8	325	66	84					1	19	8	9	13	21	
	08	2	5	1	8	259	111	48							8	24	8	21	
	10	4	2	3	12	188	14	48					1	12	14	1	8	9	
	14	2	2	6	9	238	100	48					1	25	1	41	8	21	
	15		4	1	11	285	76	60							14	32	10	20	
CODE 96 TOTAL UNITS		17	16	15	59	1686	566	408	16				5	100	75	16	65	140	
TOTAL DOLLARS		468	320	188	1099	23005	7656	6528											
90 CLASS TOTALS PRICE LINE-ALL	01	108	154	302	884	7673	2394	1192					11	28	264	24	140	404	90
	05	67	131	93	362	3475	1636	958					8	20	172	22	109	281	
	08	30	121	67	258	3054	1136	906					3	7	112	41	107	219	
	10	65	118	65	317	2680	1072	708	12				7	18	107	15	79	186	
	14	49	56	72	225	2609	1162	796					5	12	114	24	91	205	
	15	69	92	86	327	3610	1319	792	14				6	16	135	22	87	222	
CLASS 90 TOTAL UNITS		388	672	685	2373	23101	8719	5352	42				40	100	905	23	612	1516	
TOTAL DOLLARS		3965	6019	5385	20605	239725	84680	77191											
99 INVALID CODES PRICE LINE-ALL	01				1	3	52	530			29				62–		80	18	99
	05	1–	1–		3	33–	84	378					13		5–	62	58	53	
	08			2	1	31–	35	378									58	59	
	10		3		4	20–	53	378								2	58	58	
	14	1–	1–	1–	3	84	70	378					24		10–	25	58	48	
	15		1–	2	2	19–	29	378					63		7–		58	51	
CODE 99 TOTAL UNITS		2–	1	2	330–	16–	183	2420			29		1–	100	84–	133	372	288	
TOTAL DOLLARS		62–	10–	37–		4875–	3751	37204			638–								

FIGURE 23. CLASSIFICATION-STOCK STATUS REPORT

		TWO MONTHS PRIOR				ONE MONTH PRIOR				CURRENT MONTH					ONE MONTH FUTURE				
		OPENING STOCK	SALES	M/D	RECEIPT	OPENING STOCK	SALES	M/D	RECEIPT	OPENING STOCK	SALES	M/D	RECEIPT	ENDING STOCK / ON ORDER / OTB ||| OPENING STOCK	SALES	M/D	RECEIPT	ON ORDER / OTB
WEEK	LY																				
	TY																				
MONTH	TO DATE													O.O. |||				O.O.
	PLAN													OTB |||				OTB
	REV PLAN													|||				
	LAST YEAR													|||				

82 BRUSHED DENIM JEANS — DIVISION

		OS	SALES	M/D	RCPT	OS	SALES	M/D	RCPT	OS	SALES	M/D	RCPT	END/OO/OTB	OS	SALES	M/D	RCPT	OO/OTB
MONTH	TO DATE	106.0	88.4	1.8	57.6	80.1	18.6	2.4	18.7	132.1	9.3		-.4	122.4 O.O.	122.4	55.0		60.0	62.6 O.O.
	PLAN	112.1	73.0		28.4	67.5	15.0			123.9	35.5	1.7	36.4		159.0				
	REV PLAN									90.0	26.0		95.0						OTB
	LAST YEAR		-.1			.1	.1		11.8	11.7	3.5		28.6	36.0 OTB	38.6	25.1		33.4	34.0

83 BRUSHED DENIM TOPS — DIVISION

		OS	SALES	M/D	RCPT	OS	SALES	M/D	RCPT	OS	SALES	M/D	RCPT	END/OO/OTB	OS	SALES	M/D	RCPT	OO/OTB
MONTH	TO DATE	73.6	47.3	1.7	12.6	33.9	6.1	1.1	25.1	65.5	4.5		-.2	60.8 O.O.	60.8	15.0		19.0	4.9 O.O.
	PLAN	73.8	49.0		20.2	45.0	9.9			57.8	17.5	.4	21.3		80.0				
	REV PLAN									50.0	10.0		40.0	OTB					OTB
	LAST YEAR		-.1			-.1			2.7	2.7	1.6		9.4	19.2	10.9	13.4		14.0	32.4

TOTAL DENIM TOPS & JEANS

		OS	SALES	M/D	RCPT	OS	SALES	M/D	RCPT	OS	SALES	M/D	RCPT	END/OO/OTB	OS	SALES	M/D	RCPT	OO/OTB
MONTH	TO DATE	278.1	172.1	9.0	99.3	200.5	34.7	10.0	129.4	280.1	17.5		-.8	261.7 O.O.	261.7	92.0		104.0	141.9 O.O.
	PLAN	261.8	171.4		78.6	169.0	35.0		6.8	279.9	67.5	9.5	60.4		349.0				
	REV PLAN									225.0	49.0		173.0	OTB					OTB
	LAST YEAR	50.9	18.7	2.1	5.1	35.7	9.4	1.2	34.0	51.6	18.2	.6	62.3	87.3	98.3	63.1	.3	98.2	49.4

221

FIGURE 24. MONTHLY SALES AND STOCK REPORT

DEPT 20 MONTHLY SALES AND STOCK REPORT   MONTH ENDING 04/03

CODE NO	CODE DESCRIPTION	STORE	LAST YEAR 03/78 DOLLAR SALES	THIS YEAR DOLLARS SALES	THIS YEAR DOLLARS ON HAND	THIS YEAR DOLLARS ON ORDER	THIS YEAR UNITS SALES	THIS YEAR UNITS ON HAND	THIS YEAR UNITS ON ORDER	APRIL DOLLARS	APRIL UNITS	LAST YEAR SALES MAY DOLLARS	MAY UNITS	JUNE DOLLARS	JUNE UNITS	CODE NO
00	HOSIERY	01		211-	77		4-	15								00
		05		104-	87		16-	23								
		08		89-	8		4-	11								
		10		40-			1-	5								
		14		38-	13		1	6								
		15		121-	2		4-	10								
CODE 00 TOTAL				603-	187		28-	70								
91	CLASS SLIPPERS, ETC	01	1521	4944	6461	6740	1632	2507	2228	2062	767	3640	1235	2579	905	01
		05	1505	2869	4790	5502	1129	1698	1832	1292	456	2460	796	1686	617	
		08	880	1864	2632	2888	570	814	954	1017	396	1791	740	1315	523	
		10	853	1127	2529	3115	397	812	1086	754	273	1656	640	1641	658	
		14	766	1590	3098	2493	596	1063	846	803	290	1627	575	1241	479	
		15	2290	3898	7245	6214	1841	2607	2090	2616	1257	4443	1614	2884	1119	
CODE 01 TOTAL			7815	16292	26755	26952	6165	9501	9036	8544	3439	15797	5600	11346	4301	
20	CLASS BODY SUITS	01	2652	1621	9360	4591	283	1651	1620	2700	510	3064	578	1932	365	20
		05	1206	1069	5726	2828	194	903	1200	1285	238	1711	356	1289	259	
		08	1250	697	4240	2525	137	737	960	1278	240	1516	281	886	174	
		10	1739	833	3808	3403	148	622	1152	1756	332	1530	280	907	179	
		14	1293	726	4688	2665	180	900	996	1254	240	1334	254	716	137	
		15	1406	960	7125	2828	190	1155	1092	1172	220	2096	398	1228	222	
CODE 20 TOTAL			9546	5906	34947	18840	1132	5968	7020	9445	1780	11251	2147	6958	1336	
30	CLASS SOCKS & PEDS	01	6524	5922	22754	6482	6428	21366	7040	7190	8131	11957	14081	8023	9633	30
		05	5403	4673	13684	7726	4866	13310	8580	5936	7025	7683	9494	5465	6241	
		08	3576	3008	11222	4349	3076	10752	4780	3692	4043	4578	5312	3117	3753	
		10	3196	2781	11776	4411	2752	10944	4750	2998	3342	3902	4316	2630	3109	
		14	3015	2824	12323	3837	2113	11571	4240	3490	3963	4547	5446	2784	3389	
		15	3841	3469	13338	5035	3508	12582	5480	4204	4749	6311	7547	4030	4842	
CODE 30 TOTAL			25555	22677	85097	31840	23438	80625	34870	27510	31253	38978	46196	26048	30967	
40	CLASS PANTY HOSE	01						1		5	2		1-		1-	40
CODE 40 TOTAL								1		5	2		1-		1-	
42	FLAT STITCH SHEER PANTY HOSE	01	6157	5475	11462	14346	4454	8999	10140	3577	2951	6817	5262	5282	4056	42

222

FIGURE 25. STYLE PERFORMANCE RECORD

S T Y L E   P E R F O R M A N C E   R E C O R D   FOR WEEK 1/09

DEPARTMENT 009 - SPORT SHIRTS   CLASS 16 - LSTLDKNTSSLID   REPORT PAGE # 138

VENDOR	STYLE	STORE	WKS FRM RECEIPT 1ST LST	TOTAL NET SALES	CUST RET	****SALES BY WEEK**** 4WK AGO	3WK AGO	2WK AGO	THIS WEEK	ON HAND	ON ORDER	SALES/STOCK PERCENT 4WK AGO	3WK AGO	2WK AGO	THIS WEEK	CURR STAT	RETAIL	NO. MD.
HUKAPOO SUYESTA		03-MORR	49 8	210		2	18	14	5	94	60-	02	14	12	05	S	12.00	0
		09-CHILL	49 8	530		38	47	35	10	86	166-	18	26	27	10		12.00	0
		20-SPFLD	49 8	657		73	79	19	18	39	224-	32	51	25	32	F	12.00	0
		21-DPTFD	49 8	529		33	73	25	14	59	154-	16	43	26	19		12.00	0
		24-TOMRV	0 0	0		0	0	0	0	84		00	00	00	00		12.00	0
				7790*	5*	538*	667*	345*	159*	1663*	-2314*	16*	24*	16*	09*	SLOW		0*
			02/08															
627	00702	01-NWK	21 17	329		66	24	41	30	122	0	23	11	21	20	F	13.00	0
ACRYLIC		03-MORR	17 17	199		30	39	11	6	5-	0	37	76	92	600		13.00	0
		09-CHILL	21 17	261		49	45	25	11	171	0	16	18	12	06	S	13.00	0
		20-SPFLD	21 17	190		45	19	9	4	98	0	26	15	08	04	S	13.00	0
		21-DPTFD	21 17	241		60	64	18	7	119	0	22	31	13	06	S	13.00	0
				4661*	87*	909*	625*	272*	172*	1459*	0*	26*	25*	14*	11*			0*
			08/22															

STORE TOTALS UNITS FOR CLASS 16

	4WK AGO	3WK AGO	2WK AGO	THIS WEEK	ON HAND	ON ORDER	4WK AGO	3WK AGO	2WK AGO	THIS WEEK
01-NWK	206*	119*	213*	79*	507*	144*	18*	13*	27*	13*
03-MORR	61*	88*	39*	35*	189*	1*	15*	25*	15*	16*
09-CHILL	167*	169*	104*	42*	318*	-36*	21*	27*	22*	12*
20-SPFLD	209*	155*	61*	52*	388*	-136*	24*	24*	12*	12*
21-DPTFD	145*	219*	63*	34*	252*	-60*	20*	38*	18*	12*
24-TOMRV	0*	0*	0*	0*	0*	84*	00*	00*	00*	00*

CLASS TOTALS UNITS ---- 2709* 2464* 1313* 815* 6690* -747* 19* 22* 15* 11*

STORE TOTALS DOLLARS FOR CLASS 16

STORE	4WK AGO	3WK AGO	2WK AGO	THIS WEEK	ON HAND	ON ORDER	4WK AGO	3WK AGO	2WK AGO	THIS WEEK
01-NWK	3.2*	1.8*	3.4*	1.3*	7.5*	2.7*	19*	13*	28*	15*
03-MORR	.8*	1.2*	.5*	.5*	2.7*	.1*	14*	24*	14*	17*
09-CHILL	2.4*	2.4*	1.4*	.6*	4.1*	-.3*	22*	28*	24*	13*
20-SPFLD	3.1*	2.2*	.9*	.8*	6.4*	-1.5*	23*	21*	11*	11*
21-UPTFD	2.0*	3.1*	.9*	.5*	3.4*	-.6*	20*	40*	18*	12*
24-TOMRV	.0*	.0*	.0*	.0*	.0*	1.0*	00*	00*	00*	00*

CLASS TOTALS DOLLARS ---- 39.0* 35.6* 19.2* 12.3* 99.1* -5.4* 19* 21* 15* 11*

FIGURE 26. FASHION STYLE STATUS REPORT IN UNITS

DEPT 20 — FASHION STYLE STATUS REPORT IN UNITS — WEEK ENDING 04/03

CODE NO	VENDOR	STYLE	RETAIL	STORE	LAST 3 DAYS ENDING	THIS WEEK ENDING	ONE WEEK AGO ENDING	2 WEEKS AGO ENDING	LAST 4 WEEKS ENDING	SEASON TO DATE	ON HAND	ON ORDER	RECEIPT FIRST DATE	RECEIPT LAST DATE	CUST. RETURNS	NOTES	CODE NO
46	3878	6553	2.48	05		1			1	1	1-		000000	000000			
46	3878	6553	2.48	15			1		1	1	1-		000000	000000			
		STYLE TOTAL				1	1		2	2	2-						
46	3878	7550	2.48	01		56	76		132	132	139	200	030575	031776			
46	3878	7550	2.48	05		21	64		85	85	5-	60	030176	031776			
46	3878	7550	2.48	08		22	19		41	41	14	60	030176	031776			
46	3878	7550	2.48	10		15	12		27	28	28	60	030176	031776			
46	3878	7550	2.48	14		7	3		10	10	45	60	030176	031776			
46	3878	7550	2.48	15		17	19		36	36	29	60	030176	031776			
		STYLE TOTAL				138	193		331	331	250	500					
46	3878	7552	2.48	01		311	304		615	615	202	800	030575	031776			
46	3878	7552	2.48	05		152	104		256	256	67	150	030575	031776			
46	3878	7552	2.48	08		60	54		114	114	86	150	030575	031776			
46	3878	7552	2.48	10		29	36		65	65	135	150	030176	031776			
46	3878	7552	2.48	14		29	24		53	53	147	150	030176	030176			
46	3878	7552	2.48	15		90	68		158	158	117	150	030176	031776			
		STYLE TOTAL				671	590		1261	1261	754	1550					
46	3878	7555	2.48	01			2		2	2	2-	800	000000	000000			
		STYLE TOTAL					2		2	2	2-	1500					
46	3878	7557	2.48	01		175	175		350	350	507	200	030575	031776			
46	3878	7557	2.48	05		46	30		76	76	219	50	031776	021776			
46	3878	7557	2.48	08		17	15		32	32	148	50	030176	031776			
46	3878	7557	2.48	10		9	8		17	17	163	50	030176	031776			
46	3878	7557	2.48	14		16	4		20	20	160	50	030176	031776			
46	3878	7557	2.48	15		39	31		70	70	200	50	030176	031776			
		STYLE TOTAL				302	263		565	565	1397	450					
46	3878	7575	2.48	08		158	96		254	254	507						
		STYLE TOTAL				158	96		254	254	507						
46	3878	7599	2.48	01		104	64		168	168	208		030575	031776			
46	3878	7599	2.48	05		15	10		25	25	25		030176	031776			
46	3878	7599	2.48	08		14	5		19	19	46		030176	031776			
46	3878	7599	2.48	10		8	9		17	17	48		031776	031776			
46	3878	7599	2.48	14		1	4		5	5	60		030176	031776			
46	3878	7599	2.48	15		16	4		20	20	70		030176	031776			
		STYLE TOTAL				158	96		254	254	507						
46	3878	7553	2.50	01			2		2		23		030575	011576			
46	3878	7553	2.48	05							2-		000000	000000			
		STYLE TOTAL					2		2		21						
46	3878	7556	2.50	08							1		000000	000000			
		STYLE TOTAL									1						
46	3878	7559	2.50	01		14	16		30	30	249		030575	022576			
46	3878	7559	2.50	08							3-		030575	100875			
		STYLE TOTAL				14	16		30	30	246						
46	3878	7875	2.50	01						30	30		000000	000000			
		STYLE TOTAL								30	30						

224

II. REPORTS USED FOR DOLLAR CONTROL

The purpose of these reports is to provide the buyer with information on the actual performance and any variance from the planned performance. This information requires analysis for appropriate action and decisions. These reports provide the basis for dollar control of inventories.

A. Total Department Merchandise Statistics Report

The function of this report is to provide the buyer with information on the current operating status of the *total department*. The elements which affect profit are included as well as the status of the size of the stock, the sales trend and the open-to-buy amount. This type of information controls the dollar stock and helps the buyer to make adjustments when and where needed in order to insure a profitable season. The following reports (Figures 27 and 28) serve the same function, but vary in format.

B. Individual Store Merchandise Statistics Report

This report (Figure 29) provides the current operation status of the *individual stores* in a multi-store operation. It aids in the monitoring of the desired stock-sales ratio for each unit.

FIGURE 27. TOTAL DEPARTMENT MERCHANDISE STATISTICS REPORT

WEEKLY AND CUMULATIVE MERCHANDISE STATISTICS DEPT 44 BOYS CLOTHING

DATE 04/23   PLAN TO 2.34

DATE	DOLLAR SALES					DOLLAR STOCK		OPEN ORDERS				STOCK PLUS OPEN ORDERS	OPEN TO BUY		MARKUP %				MARKDOWN $ MONTH TO DATE		MARKDOWN % MONTH TO DATE		GROSS PROFIT % MONTH TO DATE	
	MERCHANDISE PLAN	Pt.+5%	THIS YEAR	% MDSE PLAN	LAST YEAR	% LAST YEAR	PLAN	THIS YEAR	PAST DUE	THIS MONTH	NEXT MONTH	SUBSEQUENT MONTH		THIS MONTH	THIS MONTH + NEXT MONTH	M-T-O PURCHASES	STOCK	PLAN	THIS YEAR	PLAN	THIS YEAR	PLAN	THIS YEAR	PLAN	THIS YEAR
LAST QUARTER	490.0	514.5	432.3	-11.8	480.5	-10.0	173.0	166.5	3.0	162.9	76.2	27.5	438.2	-27.5	51.3	50.9			40.3		1.9		18.1		29.5
WEEK 1	8.6	9.0	10.3	19.3	8.5	20.2		196.1		193.1	84.4	27.5	480.3	-71.8	-1.2	42.1			40.2		9.0		37.2		17.9
WEEK 2	10.4	10.9	13.9	33.9	10.5	33.0		202.8		159.8	103.3	27.5	439.9	-24.8	26.9	36.4			38.9		9.5		25.8		23.1
WEEK 3	12.3	12.9	12.5	2.0	12.4	.8		176.8		139.3	121.5	115.1	448.5	-27.9	5.6	37.9			39.1		11.7		22.5		25.5
WEEK 4	12.7	13.3	15.3	21.1	12.8	20.0		187.8	84.8	108.1	15.9	101.5	476.0	-27.9	25.2										
WEEK 5	14.1	14.8	12.9	-8.2	14.0	-8.1		267.2						-20.1		39.1			39.4		13.4		20.6		26.9
MONTH	58.1	61.0	64.9	12.0	58.2	11.5	285.0	303.2	10.3	98.5	9.5	101.5	431.6	1.4	53.1	39.9	39.8	39.8	39.4	8.8	13.4	15.1	20.6	30.7	26.9
WEEK 1	26.5	27.8	19.1	-28.1	18.7	1.8		333.3	1.1	146.3	19.2	101.5	499.9	-105.6	-63.6	20.4			40.1		1.1		5.8		36.6
WEEK 2	38.5	40.4	26.2	-31.9	24.7	6.0		404.2		34.8	41.1	101.5	480.1	-115.9	-95.8	40.3			40.0		1.8		4.0		37.6
WEEK 3	51.9	54.5	37.9	-26.9	36.7	3.3		370.7	13.3	62.0	4.3	97.2	450.3	-128.8	-84.1	40.7			40.3		3.4		4.1		37.9
WEEK 4	67.0	80.3	59.2	-11.6	49.8	18.8										41.8			41.0		4.8		3.3		39.0
MONTH	184.0	193.2	142.4	-22.5	130.0	9.5	256.0	273.7		31.5	4.3	97.2	309.5	-65.9	-21.2	39.9	39.8	39.8	41.0	7.9	4.8	4.3	3.3	37.2	39.0
WEEK 1	78.0	81.9	101.6	30.3	65.4	55.2		259.8		22.0	4.3	97.2	286.0	-57.4	-12.7	27.4			39.9		.8		.8		39.5
WEEK 2	14.9	15.6	20.6	38.1	73.0	-71.8		232.9		16.2	4.3	97.2	253.4	-37.7	7.0	27.6			39.5		4.2		4.2		37.4
WEEK 3	13.0	13.6	12.7	-1.9	10.8	18.0										29.5			39.5		22.6		16.8		29.4
WEEK 4	13.1	13.8			11.0																				
MONTH	119.2	125.2	134.9	27.4	160.0	-9.6	198.0									39.9	39.8	39.8	39.5	9.8	22.6	8.2	16.8	34.9	29.4
SEASON-TO-DATE	347.7	365.0	342.2	-1.6	337.5	1.4										40.2			40.0		40.8		11.9		32.9
SEASON	497.2	522.1			478.2											39.9	39.8		39.5	47.2		9.5		34.1	

MONTHLY PLAN MU ON PURCHASE IS SHOWN ON MONTH LINES AND SEASON LINE

MONTHLY STATISTICS

	UNIT SALES THIS YEAR	$ AVERAGE SALE				% CUST RETS		TURNOVER				WEEKS SUPPLY
		THIS YEAR	LAST YEAR					PLAN	THIS YEAR			
MONTH 1	4.0	16.05	16.30			13.6		.34	.33			5
MONTH 2	6.8	20.88	19.76			9.5		.65	.53			24
MONTH 3			21.34					.47				
SEASON-TO-DATE	17.0	20.17	20.18			11.7		1.46	1.23			

FIGURE 28. TOTAL DEPARTMENT MERCHANDISE STATISTICS REPORT

FIGURE 29. INDIVIDUAL STORE MERCHANDISE STATISTICS REPORT

C. Operating Statement

Large stores periodically prepare a statement for each merchandise department which itemizes and recapitulates the relationships of all factors affecting profit and/or loss. The report which reveals the profit position of a department is called an OPERATING STATEMENT. Operating statements are generally prepared monthly for each department and then combined into a final statement. The monthly statements are primarily designed to furnish gross margin information as well as other statistics which permit a careful analysis and which act as a guide for improving performance. This technique permits the buyer to evaluate and improve his operation of a department because it:

- shows the relationships of profit factors;
- reveals the effects on profits caused by changes;
- permits comparison with other departments and other stores by means of percentages.

The use of computers permits ongoing operating statements. The form of an operating statement varies in different stores as does the amount of information presented, but the elements shown in the following illustration are typical of the information included.

FIGURE 30. MERCHANDISE OPERATING STATEMENT

		4 WEEKS ENDED				5 WEEKS ENDED			
		THIS YEAR		LAST YEAR		THIS YEAR		LAST YEAR	
		AMOUNT	%	AMOUNT	%	AMOUNT	%	AMOUNT	%
# TRANSACTIONS & AVG. SALE	1								
CUSTOMERS RETURNS & %	2								
% CASH DISC. TO COST PURCH.	3								
RETAIL PURCHASES & MU%	4								
RETAIL STOCK END PERIOD & MU%	5								
MARKDOWNS	6								
SHORTAGES	7								
EMPLOYEES' DISCOUNT	8								
NET SALES PERIOD & % INCREASE	9								
NET SALES-YEAR TO DATE & % INC.	10								
ALTERATION COST	11								
OTHER COST OF SALES	12								
GROSS MARGIN & % TO SALES	13								
CASH DISCOUNT & % TO COST	14								
GROSS MARGIN PLUS DISCOUNT-PERIOD	15								
GROSS MARGIN PLUS DISCOUNT-YEAR	16								
MERCHANDISE SALARIES & EXPENSE	17								
SALESPEOPLES' SALARIES & COMM.	18								
STOCK & MISC. DIRECT SALARIES	19								
PAYROLL TAX & EMPLOYEE BENEFITS	20								
NEWSPAPER ADVERTISING	21								
DIRECT MAIL & MAGAZINE ADV.	22								
ADVERTISING PREPARATION	23								
WINDOWS AND SIGNS	24								
WRAPPING	25								
DELIVERY	26								
MERCHANDISE ADJUSTMENTS	27								
SELLING SUPPLIES, ETC.	28								
RENT	29								
OCCUPANCY & HOUSEKEEPING	30								
INTEREST & INSURANCE ON MERCH.	31								
TOTAL CONTROLLABLE EXPENSES	32								
DEPARTMENT CONTRIBUTION	33								
INDIRECT EXPENSE	34								
TOTAL EXPENSE	35								
OPERATING PROFIT-PERIOD	36								
OPERATING PROFIT-YEAR TO DATE	37								

To understand the operation, it is necessary to analyze each item listed and then interpret the results. It is possible to compare a current merchandise operating statement with last year's statement for the same period as a means of measuring changes in performance either for a specific single factor or the total picture. In addition, there are several annual statistical reports (expressed in percentages) used by retailers for purposes of comparing operations. The best known is the Merchandising and Operating Results, called MOR, published annually by the National Retail Merchants Association to which retailers contribute figures which are then collated and published.

The interpretation of the operating factors in the order in which they appear on the sample form (Figure 30) are:

1. Number of transactions and average sale.

    a. Indicates the number of customers the department is servicing in a given period
    b. Indicates the actual dollar amount of the average transaction in the department
    c. Reveals trend in price levels of department

2. Customer returns and percentage.

    a. Expressed as the percentage of customer returns to gross sales
    b. Measures efficiency of retaining sales originally made

3. Percent cash discount to cost purchase.

    a. Indicates the amount of cash discounts earned based on the cost of goods
    b. Controlling this factor is important since it frequently represents the difference between profit and loss
    c. Measures ability to take advantage of terms

4. Retail purchases and markup percent.

    a. Shows the result or accumulation of all initial markons for period to date
    b. Helps achieve desired markup needed

5. Retail stock end period and markup percent.

    a. Indicates quantity of stock on hand at a retail value, and the MU%
    b. Helps in achieving profitable MU% at end of period

6. Markdowns.

    a. Indicates amount ($ and %) taken to date
    b. Analysis of amounts:

       - Helps prevent an excessive percentage of markdowns
       - Able to investigate the reason(s) for excess
       - Prevents reducing the final gross margin to a low level

7. Shortages.

   a. In monthly statements, shortage given is *estimated* difference between the book and the actual physical inventory
   b. Does not change monthly, but is included in the calculation of the final gross margin percentage
   c. Shortage percentages reflect buyer's ability because buyer is responsible for them

8. Employee discount.

   a. Cumulation of the amount of employee discounts given to date
   b. Affects gross margin in the same manner as the other retail reductions

9. Net sales period and percent increase.

   a. Shows dollar sales realized for period and the percentage of change
   b. Shows trend of a department's business

10. Net sales—year to date and percent increase.

    a. Shows dollar sales realized up to date
    b. Aggregate figure for the period

11. Alteration cost.

    a. Reduces the gross margin
    b. Charged against the parent selling departments

12. Other cost of sales.

    a. Affects gross margin the same way as markdowns
    b. Accounts for inward transportation of goods

13. Gross margin and percent to sales.

    a. Shows the amount resulting from the subtraction of the total cost of goods from net sales
    b. Expressed also as a percentage of net sales

14. Cash discount and percent to sales.

    a. Indicates the dollar amount and its percentage relationship to net sales of discounts earned and deducted from billed costs
    b. Lower than accepted trade discounts should not be accepted

15. Gross margin plus discount for the period.

    a. Shows the amount of gross margin for the period
    b. Includes the cash discount amounts

16. Gross margin plus discount for the year.

    a. Shows the amount of gross margin for the year
    b. Includes the cash discount amounts

17 to 31. Direct expenses.

    a. Various direct expenses, listed by classification, which affect the sales volume
    b. Expressed as a percentage of net sales

32. Total controllable expenses.

    a. Sum total of all direct departmental expenses

33. Department contribution.

    a. Obtained by deducting the "direct" operating expenses from the gross margin
    b. Considered to be the direct responsibility of the buyer

34. Indirect expense.

    a. Expenses that continue to exist even if department is discontinued
    b. Not considered to be a direct responsibility of the buyer

35. Total expense.

    a. A summary of all expenses of operating the department
    b. Combination of direct and indirect expenses

36. Operating profit for the period.

37. Operating profit for the year to date.

    a. Issued semi-annually or annually
    b. Comparative with last year and indicates a trend
    c. Denotes what is left of sales income after deducting both the cost of sales and operating expenses

D. **Profit and Loss Statement**
This financial statement shows the net profit of a merchandise department. This is generally issued at the end of the season or year. It should not be a revelation—it should confirm what a merchandiser already knows about the performance of the department.

FIGURE 31. DEPARTMENTAL PROFIT AND LOSS STATEMENT

DEPARTMENTAL PROFIT AND LOSS	AMOUNT IN 100'S	%	ANNUAL 1979 AMOUNT IN 100'S	%	ANNUAL 1978 AMOUNT IN 100'S	%	AMOUNT IN 100'S	%
NET SALES-DIVISION			3,765.8		3,539.3			
MARKON				37.5		37.3		
MARKDOWN				6.7		6.2		
SHORTAGE AT RETAIL				5.7		4.7		
MAINTAINED MARKON			1,119.9	29.7	1,079.1	30.5		
DISCOUNT EARNED			212.0	5.6	196.2	5.5		
ALTERATION/OTHER ADJUSTMENT			-.4		-4.0	-.1		
GROSS MARGIN			1,331.5	35.4	1,271.3	35.9		
SELLING SALARIES			331.9	8.8	322.9	9.1		
RECEIVING AND RESERVE			53.5	1.4	52.9	1.5		
WRAPPING AND PACKING			37.9	1.0	30.3	.9		
DELIVERY			24.2	.6	18.1	.5		
OTHER Q			57.4	1.5	50.2	1.4		
TOTAL Q			504.9	13.4	474.4	13.4		
NEWSPAPER SPACE-NET			70.3	1.9	55.6	1.6		
DIRECT MAIL-NET			1.4		-19.5	-.6		
OTHER PUBLICITY			17.8	.5	-.7			
TOTAL PUBLICITY			89.4	2.4	35.4	1.0		
BUYING LINE			68.7	1.8	57.7	1.6		
MERCHANDISE SELLING LINE			95.7	2.5	81.0	2.3		
MERCHANDISE CONTROL			12.8	.3	8.6	.2		
TRAVEL/MISCELLANEOUS			16.4	.4	13.4	.4		
PAYROLL LOADS			107.3	2.8	97.5	2.8		
INTEREST AND TAXES ON INVENTORY			62.4	1.7	55.9	1.6		
TOTAL OPERATING EXPENSES			957.6	25.4	823.9	23.3		
DEPARTMENT MARGIN			373.9	9.9	447.4	12.6		
RENT AND OCCUPANCY			214.2	5.7	177.0	5.0		
GENERAL OVERHEAD			184.4	4.9	169.6	4.8		
DEPT. PROFIT OR LOSS			-24.7	-.7	100.8	2.8		

NET SALES & % TO TOTAL STORE							SALES/SQ.FT.		SELLING AREA-IN 100's	
							TY	LY	TY	LY
STORE 01			490.0	1.09	554.7	1.21	212	254	2.3	2.2
STORE 02			399.3	.75	384.6	.73	271	261	1.5	1.5
STORE 03			383.6	.95	377.2	.93	208	205	1.8	1.8
STORE 04			326.9	.89	295.4	.84	219	229	1.5	1.3
STORE 05			280.6	.89	284.9	.88	260	258	1.1	1.1
STORE 06			244.1	.71	257.1	.78	250	256	1.0	1.0
STORE 07			210.5	.81	247.8	.91	163	194	1.3	1.3
STORE 08			188.6	.72	206.8	.83	176	193	1.1	1.1
STORE 09			204.4	.84	184.0	.75	171	154	1.2	1.2
STORE 10			155.7	.72	147.8	.69	131	124	1.2	1.2
STORE 11			231.9	1.11	193.2	1.09	255	212	.9	.9
STORE 12			137.1	1.13	152.9	1.23	138	154	1.0	1.0
STORE 13			109.7	.92	106.3	.90	119	134	.9	.8
STORE 14			48.0	.89	58.2	.90	64	78	.8	.8
STORE 15			150.1	.71	88.4	.72	157	185	1.0	.5
STORE 16										
STORE 17										.2
STORE 18			114.3	.60			113		1.2	
STORE 19			89.9	.78			277		.4	

STATISTICAL DATA

	AMOUNT	PCT.
STOCK TURN		
1979		2.4
1978		2.5
AVERAGE CHECK		
1979	19.76	
1978	21.61	
% RETURNS/GROSS SALES		
1979		7.7
1978		8.6
GROSS TRANS-INC. COD		
1979	206.6	
1978	179.3	
% SENT TRANS.		
1979		11.4
1978		19.2

NOTES

APPENDIX

The Use of Basic Arithmetic in Merchandising

Numbers are the language of business. In merchandising, numbers are used in buying activities, selling activities, and in interpreting and analyzing figures from records involved in performing these functions. Basic arithmetic is used in solving merchandising problems faced by the salesperson, the buyer, and the merchandise manager. At every level, the knowledge of these basic arithmetic processes is an essential skill. Merchandising decisions are based on numerical facts; merchandising concepts and successes are also expressed in numbers.

To develop a greater appreciation of number relationships, resulting in a better understanding of the mathematical factors involved in merchandising profitably, the fundamental operations of fractions, decimals and percentages will be briefly explained and then reviewed through their application to actual merchandising situations.

I. FRACTIONS

A FRACTION is a way of expressing a part of a whole quantity, such as $3/4$ of the shipment or $7/10$ of the dresses. The number above the line is called the NUMERATOR, and the number below the line is called the DENOMINATOR. The line in a fraction means "divided by," as $3/4$ means 3 divided by 4.

When the fraction has a value of less than 1, as $3/4$ and $7/10$, it is called a PROPER FRACTION. In this type of fraction, the numerator is *less* than the denominator.

When the fraction has a value of one or more, as $4/3$ and $10/7$, it is called an IMPROPER FRACTION. In this type of fraction, the numerator is *greater* than the denominator.

When the number is composed of a whole number and a fraction, $3\frac{1}{8}$ and $2\frac{4}{5}$, it is called a MIXED NUMBER.

In some computations it may be necessary to *change an improper fraction to a mixed number form*. This is done by dividing the numerator by the denominator and writing the remainder, if any, as a fraction.

EXAMPLES:

$$\frac{4}{3} = 3\overline{)4} = 1\frac{1}{3}$$

$$\frac{10}{7} = 7\overline{)10} = 1\frac{3}{7}$$

When it is necessary to *change a mixed number to an improper fraction,* multiply the denominator by the whole number, add the numerator, and place the results over the denominator.

EXAMPLES:

$$3\frac{1}{8} = \frac{(8 \times 3) + 1}{8} = \frac{24 + 1}{8} = \frac{25}{8}$$

$$2\frac{4}{5} = \frac{(5 \times 2) + 4}{5} = \frac{10 + 4}{5} = \frac{14}{5}$$

The *addition and subtraction of fractions* require converting all fractions to fractions having the same denominator. This is called a COMMON DENOMINATOR. The *common denominator* of *two or more* numbers is a number that is *exactly divisible* by each of them.

EXAMPLE: 12 is the common denominator of $\frac{2}{3}$ and $\frac{3}{4}$

Finding a common denominator entails CHANGING FRACTIONS TO HIGHER TERMS. Fractions can be raised by *multiplying the numerator and the denominator by the same number.*

PROBLEM: Raise $\frac{2}{3}$ to twelfths; raise $\frac{3}{4}$ to twelfths.

SOLUTION: $\frac{2 \times 4}{3 \times 4} = \frac{8}{12}$

$\frac{3 \times 3}{4 \times 3} = \frac{9}{12}$

To simplify the work, it is desirable to use the LEAST COMMON DENOMINATOR of the series of fractions. The *lowest common denominator means using one smallest denominator* that can be *divided evenly* by all denominators. It is abbreviated LCD. When one denominator can be divided evenly by the other, the LCD is found *by inspection*.

EXAMPLE: For $\frac{3}{4}$ and $\frac{1}{8}$, the LCD is 8 since it can be divided evenly by 4 and 8

When the *denominators have no common denominators*, the LCD is found by *multiplying the denominators.*

PROBLEM: For $\frac{2}{3}, \frac{4}{7}$ and $\frac{3}{5}$, what is the LCD?
SOLUTION: $3 \times 7 \times 5 = 105$ (LCD)

As a rule, a fraction should be reduced to its LOWEST TERMS. A fraction is reduced to its lowest terms when *no whole number can be divided evenly into both the numerator and the denominator*. To reduce the fraction to its lowest terms, divide the numerator and the denominator by the same number or numbers until *no number can be found that divides into both evenly.*

PROBLEM: Reduce $\frac{36}{60}$ to its lowest terms.

SOLUTION: $\frac{36}{60} = \frac{36 \div 4}{60 \div 4} = \frac{9}{15} = \frac{9 \div 3}{15 \div 3} = \frac{3}{5}$

or

$\frac{36}{60} = \frac{36 \div 12}{60 \div 12} = \frac{3}{5}$

A. Adding Fractions

In the addition of fractions, the *denominators* of all fractions must be changed to *the same common denominator*. The *final answer* should *be reduced* and expressed in the *lowest terms*.

CONCEPT: Addition of fractions = $\dfrac{\text{Total of the numerators}}{\text{Least common denominator}}$

PROBLEM: The salesperson in the yard goods department sold to one customer ½ yard of blue ribbon and ¼ yard of pink ribbon. How much ribbon was purchased by this customer?

SOLUTION:

$$\dfrac{1}{2} = \dfrac{2}{4}$$
$$+\dfrac{1}{4} = \dfrac{1}{4}$$

Common denominator

$$\dfrac{3}{4} \text{ of a yard}$$

B. Subtracting Fractions

In the subtraction of fractions, the denominators of all fractions must be changed to the *same common denominator*. The answer should be expressed in its *lowest terms*.

CONCEPT: Subtraction of fractions = $\dfrac{\text{Difference between the numerators}}{\text{Least common denominator}}$

PROBLEM: Store X received a shipment of 48 suits. Five-sixths (⅚) of the shipment was transferred to Store Y which, in turn, transferred ½ of its shipment to Store Z. What fractional part of the shipment was retained by Store Y?

SOLUTION:

$$\dfrac{5}{6} = \dfrac{5}{6}$$
$$-\dfrac{1}{2} = \dfrac{3}{6}$$

Common denominator

$$\dfrac{2}{6} = \dfrac{1}{3} \text{ (Lowest terms) of shipment}$$

NOTES

PRACTICE PROBLEMS

1. On June 6, the upholstery department received a bolt of material $137\frac{1}{2}$ yards long. One week later, it received another bolt of the same pattern that measured $87\frac{5}{8}$ yards. How many yards were received into stock?

2. In recarpeting the children's departments of the Fram Shop, one department required $54\frac{7}{8}$ yards, another $61\frac{1}{2}$ yards, and the third required $49\frac{1}{3}$ yards. How many yards of carpeting were to be ordered?

3. It took one department $3\frac{3}{4}$ days to take a count of its entire stock. On the first day, $\frac{7}{25}$ was recorded; on the second day, another $\frac{7}{40}$ was completed; and on the third day, $\frac{7}{20}$ more was completed. What part of the counting had to be completed on the fourth day?

4. A part-time salesperson was hired to work 28 hours per week, Monday through Friday. From Monday through Thursday, he worked the following hours: $4\frac{1}{4}$, $5\frac{7}{12}$, $6\frac{3}{16}$ and $7\frac{5}{6}$. Determine the number of hours he worked on Friday.

5. A shipment of $10\frac{1}{2}$ dozen ties was to be shipped to a store. Four and one-sixth ($4\frac{1}{6}$) dozen fit into each of the first two cartons. How many dozens will be shipped in the third carton?

NOTES

C. Multiplying Fractions

In the multiplication of fractions, when *one or more of the fractions is a mixed number, it must be converted into an improper fraction before multiplying*. Though it is not necessary to find the lowest common denominator, the *multiplication of fractions* can be *simplified by cancelling before multiplying*. The final answer should be *reduced and expressed in the lowest terms*.

CONCEPT: Multiplication of fractions = $\dfrac{\text{Multiplication of numerators}}{\text{Multiplication of denominators}}$

PROBLEM: An operator who can sew $12\dfrac{4}{7}$ units an hour worked $7\dfrac{5}{12}$ hours. How many units were produced?

SOLUTION: $12\dfrac{4}{7} \times 7\dfrac{5}{12}$

$12\dfrac{4}{7} = \dfrac{88}{7}$

$7\dfrac{5}{12} = \dfrac{89}{12}$

then: $\dfrac{\cancel{88}^{22}}{7} \times \dfrac{89}{\cancel{12}_{3}} = \dfrac{22 \times 89}{7 \times 3} = \dfrac{1958}{21} = 93\dfrac{5}{21}$

D. Fractional Quantities

When a fractional quantity of something is bought, ⅚ of a yard of cloth for example, in order to find the amount of the purchase, it is *necessary to multiply the price by the fraction*.

PROBLEM: A yard of lace costs $4.75. How much would you pay for $\dfrac{5}{6}$ of a yard?

SOLUTION: $\$4.75 \times \dfrac{5}{6} = \dfrac{23.75}{6} = \$3.958 = \$3.96$

When the quantity bought is a mixed number, as 3⅔ yards, in order to find the amount of the purchase, *multiply the price of each part of the mixed number*.

PROBLEM: Find the amount of a purchase of $3\dfrac{2}{3}$ yards of ribbon @ 98¢ per yard.

SOLUTION: $.98 \times 3\dfrac{2}{3} = .98 \times \dfrac{11}{3} = \dfrac{10.78}{3} = \$3.593 = \$3.59$

When it is *necessary to convert a fractional quantity of something to a whole number*, as ½ of 180 pieces, *multiply the fraction by the whole quantity.*

EXAMPLE: $\dfrac{2}{5}$ of 40 suits

SOLUTION: $\dfrac{2}{\cancel{5}_1} \times \cancel{40}^{8} = \dfrac{16}{1} = 16$ suits

E. Dividing Fractions

In the *division of fractions*, when *mixed numbers* are used, they *should be converted into improper fractions before dividing with them*, as 7½ to ¹⁵⁄₂. When one of the numbers to *be divided is a whole number*, use *that* whole number as the numerator and *1* as the denominator. The method used for division of fractions is to *invert* the divisor, ¾ to ⁴⁄₃ for example, and multiply the inverted divisor by the dividend, using the cancellation method.

EXAMPLES: a. $7\dfrac{1}{2} \div \dfrac{1}{2}$

b. $16 \div \dfrac{3}{4}$

c. $\dfrac{3}{16} \div \dfrac{8}{9}$

SOLUTIONS: a. $7\dfrac{1}{2} \div \dfrac{1}{2} = \dfrac{15}{2} \div \dfrac{1}{2} = \dfrac{15}{\cancel{2}_1} \times \dfrac{\cancel{2}^1}{1} = \dfrac{15}{1} = 15$

b. $\dfrac{16}{1} \div \dfrac{3}{4} = 16 \times \dfrac{4}{3} = \dfrac{64}{3} = 21\dfrac{1}{3}$

c. $\dfrac{3}{16} \div \dfrac{8}{9} = \dfrac{3}{16} \times \dfrac{9}{8} = \dfrac{27}{128}$

PRACTICE PROBLEMS

1. After a rectangular-shaped department was enlarged, it measured $21\frac{3}{8}$ feet by $14\frac{4}{5}$ feet. How many square feet of space did the department contain after alteration?

2. The sportswear buyer of a major department store decided to transfer $7\frac{1}{2}$ dozen jeans to the suburban stores, which left the downtown store with $9\frac{3}{4}$ dozen jeans in stock. How many dozens had been purchased?

3. The stock of jackets in the men's department amounted to 400 pieces. If the buyer sends $\frac{3}{10}$ of them back to the manufacturer, how many jackets were returned?

4. A store sold $200,000 worth of goods in April. It sold $\frac{1}{4}$ more merchandise in May. How much did it sell in May?

5. How many pieces of $3\frac{3}{8}$ yards of fabric can be cut from a bolt that is 54 feet long?

6. Determine the total amount of a sale if Salesperson A sold the following:
   $2\frac{2}{4}$ yards @ 79¢
   $4\frac{1}{4}$ yards @ $1.35
   8 yards @ $35\frac{1}{2}$¢

NOTES

II. DECIMALS (DECIMAL FRACTIONS)

All decimals are fractions (they express values less than 1). Decimals are merely a special group of fractions, written a special way. Since decimals are so convenient to work with, it is helpful to be able to write fractions in decimal form.

When the denominator of a fraction is 10, 100, 1,000, or 10,000, etc. and you wish to express the fraction of a decimal, you can write only the *numerator of the fraction without its denominator*. The number of places at the right of the decimal point shows the value of the denominator. One decimal place means tenths; two place, hundredths; three places, thousandths, etc. When a fraction is written this way, it is called a DECIMAL FRACTION or, more commonly, a DECIMAL.

EXAMPLES: $\frac{3}{10} = .3$

$\frac{75}{100} = .75$

$\frac{245}{1000} = .245$

A. Changing a Common Fraction to Decimal Form

Any fractional number can be converted to an equivalent decimal numeral by *dividing the denominator into the numerator to as many decimal places as required*. When the decimal equivalents are not equal, such as 5/6, they should be carried to *a minimum of four decimal places for the proper accuracy*, unless the answer is expressed as a fraction.

EXAMPLE: Convert $\frac{5}{6}$ to a decimal.

SOLUTION:
$$6 \overline{)5.0000}^{.8333} \qquad \frac{5}{6} = .8333 = .83\frac{1}{3}$$

$$\begin{array}{r} \underline{48} \\ 20 \\ \underline{18} \\ 20 \\ \underline{18} \\ 20 \\ \underline{18} \\ 2 \end{array}$$

B. Changing a Decimal to a Fraction

Any decimal numeral can be converted to *an equivalent fractional numeral*. The decimal number becomes the numerator of the fraction, and the *number of places at the right of the point* shows the *value of the denominator*, e.g., one decimal place means tenths, etc. Remove the decimal point. Reduce the fraction to lowest terms.

EXAMPLE: Convert .60 to a fraction

SOLUTION: $.60 = \frac{60}{100} = \frac{3}{5}$

245

C. Adding Decimals

In the addition of decimals (whether accompanied by whole numbers or not), the decimal points *must be kept in a vertical line,* and then the column is added.

EXAMPLE: Add .68, 35.3, 5.6002, 284.45 and 7.20006

SOLUTION: .68
               35.3
               5.6002
             284.45
               7.20006
            333.23026

D. Subtracting Decimals

In the subtraction of decimals, the numbers must also be written with the decimal points in a line. The *two numbers must have the same number of decimal places, if necessary adding a cipher.*

EXAMPLE: Subtract 3.1751 from 5.952

SOLUTION: 5.9520
              −3.1751
               2.7769

E. Multiplying Decimals

When multiplying decimals, it is *necessary to point off in the product as many decimal places as there are in either* or in *both the multiplier and the multiplicand.*

EXAMPLE: Multiply $24.55 by 3.6

SOLUTION: $ 24.55 (two decimal places)
              × 3.6 (one decimal place)
              14730
              7365
           $88.380 (three decimal places)

In final answers that deal with amounts of money, numbers are usually rounded to cents. For example, if the third decimal figure is one-half cent or more, such as $88.385, the final answer would be $88.39. If it is less than one-half cent, it is dropped; $88.383 would be $88.38.

EXAMPLE: Multiply 47 by .35

SOLUTION: 47 (whole number)
               × .35 (two decimal places)
              235
              141
            16.45 (two decimal places)

F. Dividing Decimals

When a decimal is divided by a whole number, the decimal *point in the quotient is placed directly over the decimal point in the dividend.*

EXAMPLE: Divide 64 by .16

SOLUTION: .16) 64

$$.16.\overline{)64.00.} = 400.$$

If there is a remainder, it is desirable to "carry out" the quotient to 2, 3 or 4 decimal places.

EXAMPLE: Divide 59 by 2.9

SOLUTION:
```
            20.344
     2.9.)59.0.000
          58
          ---
          100
           87
          ---
          130
          116
          ---
           140
           116
           ---
            24
```

NOTES

PRACTICE PROBLEMS

1. Change the following fractions to decimal form:

    $\dfrac{7}{8}$ $\dfrac{4}{7}$ $\dfrac{3}{5}$ $\dfrac{9}{11}$ $\dfrac{2}{25}$

2. Change the following decimals to fractions:

    .064   .001   .305   1.00   .25

3. In checking the daily dollar sales of a department, the sales were: $0.86, 19.00, 10.20, 0.11, 9.99, 6.75, 20.20, 8.12, 11.01, 4.15, 2.19, 17.00, 25.26. Find the total sales.

4. The total sales of a department amounted to $1,342.38, with an average sale of $3.22. How many transactions were made?

5. During a sale, the hosiery department sold 48½ dozen pairs of pantyhose that were priced at $0.79 each. What were the total sales from this event?

NOTES

III. PERCENTAGES

The understanding of percentages is important since it is so widely utilized in business. The basis of numerous comparisons, the pricing of goods, discounts, etc. are involved with the use of percentages. Percent is just another way of writing a fraction in which the denominator is *100*. The % sign replaces the denominator and always means hundredths. For example, we can think of *8%* as *8* out of *100*.

A. Changing a Decimal to a Percent

After a fraction has been changed into a decimal, it may be written as a % *by moving the decimal point two places to the right* and adding the % sign. A whole number is converted in the same way.

EXAMPLES: $\frac{3}{4} = .75 = 75\%$

5 = 500%

B. Changing a Percent to a Fraction

To change a percent to a fraction, write the percent as a fraction whose *numerator* is the *given percent* and whose *denominator is 100*. Then reduce the fraction to lowest terms.

EXAMPLE: $35\% = \frac{35}{100} = \frac{7}{20}$

C. Changing a Percent to a Decimal

To change a percent to a decimal, *drop the % sign*, and *move the decimal point two places* to the *left*.

EXAMPLE: 20% = .20

Sometimes a percent contains a fraction. Such percents can usually be written as decimals. First, express the *fraction as a decimal;* then move the *decimal point two places to the left*.

EXAMPLES: $3\frac{1}{2}\%$ = 3.5% = .035
$2\frac{1}{4}\%$ = 2.25% = .0225

To change a *fractional percent* to a *decimal*, change the *percent* to its *own decimal form*, and then *convert* the *percent to a decimal*.

EXAMPLE: $\frac{1}{2}\%$ = .5% = .005

251

D. Basic Elements of Percent Problems
Percentage problems consider three basic elements as follows:

- *base*—the whole amount of anything, or 100%.
- *rate*—the % taken of the base.
- *percentage*—the result, or product, of multiplying the % (rate) by the whole amount (base).

EXAMPLE: 2% (R) of $900 (B) = $18 (P)
or
.02 × $900 = $18

Given any two of these elements, the third can be determined through formulas.

1. **Finding the percentage.**
   This is the most common type of percentage problem. The *whole amount* is *multiplied* by the *given %*.

   CONCEPT: Percentage = Base × Rate

   PROBLEM: 12% is deducted for taxes for your weekly salary of $125. How much, in dollars, was deducted?

   SOLUTION: P = B × R
   P = $125 × 12% = 125 × .12 = $15

2. **Finding the base.**
   The base is always the largest number since it represents the whole amount of anything. To find it, *change the % (rate) to a decimal* and *divide* it *into the product* (percentage).

   CONCEPT: $\text{Base} = \dfrac{\text{Percentage}}{\text{Rate}}$

   PROBLEM: $15, which is 12% of your salary, was deducted for taxes. How much is your salary?

   SOLUTION: $B = \dfrac{P}{R}$

   $B = \dfrac{\$15}{12\%} = \dfrac{\$15}{.12} = \$125$

3. Finding the rate.

This is used when it is necessary to express the fractional part of a whole amount as a percent. The *partial amount is the numerator* and the *whole quantity* becomes *the denominator of the fraction* which is then *converted to a percent.*

CONCEPT: $\text{Rate} = \dfrac{\text{Percentage}}{\text{Base}}$

PROBLEM: $15 dollars was deducted from your salary of $125. What % is deducted for taxes?

SOLUTION: $R = \dfrac{P}{B}$

$R = \dfrac{\$15}{\$125} = .12 = 12\%$

Certain percentage problems require the percentage to be added to the base to find the amount, or the percentage to be subtracted from the base to find the difference.

PROBLEM: Last month Department Y sold $5,000. This month they sold 15% more. How much are this month's sales?

SOLUTION: B × R = P
$5,000 (B) × 15% (R) = $750 (P)
$5,000 + $750 = $5,750

PROBLEM: A department has a stock of capes worth $2,400. Ten percent (10%) are fur-trimmed. What is the value of the untrimmed capes?

SOLUTION: B × R = P
$2,400 (B) × 10% (R) = $240 (P)
$2,400 − $240 = $2,160

NOTES

PRACTICE PROBLEMS

1. Change the following percentages to decimals:
   2%   37.5%   .4%   33⅓%   150%

2. Express each of the following in percentages *and* as fractions:
   .064   .001   3.05   1.00   .01

3. There were 200 executives working for an organization. They represented 25% of the total employees. How many exployees worked in this firm?

4. Brancn store X had sales of $8,000,000. Branch store Y had 85% of the sales produced by Store X. What were the sale of Store Y?

5. A buying office employed 105 people of whom 35 were women. What percentage of women was employed?

6. A department achieved an increase of sales amounting to $175,000. This was 12% increase over last year. What were last year's sales?

NOTES

PRACTICE PROBLEMS FOR REVIEW OF APPENDIX

1. If 1,000 skirts were sold through a newspaper promotion, and ⅛ were returned by customers, how many were returned?

2. On Saturday, 56 customers purchased fabric. Clerk A waited on ⅜ of them. How many customers did she handle?

3. A salesperson's salary was $130 weekly. One-tenth (¹⁄₁₀) was deducted for a pension fund. How much was deducted?

4. What was the total amount charged to the customer who bought 3 blouses at $9.98 each, with a sales tax of 7%?

5. A buyer in a downtown store had an inventory of $2,853 on hand December 1. On December 2, the buyer transferred the following items to the suburban store:
   30 blouses at $6.75 each
   36 blouses at $3.75 each
   24 blouses at $5.75 each
   What percentage of the inventory was transferred?

6. The handbag buyer decided to transfer 7½% of her tote bags, and 40% of her evening bag stock—dollarwise—to the suburban branch. Her tote stock was valued at $1,130, and her evening stock at $1,953. What dollar amount of goods was transferred to the branch store?

7. A dress buyer received a shipment of 50 dresses, each costing $10.75, and retailing at $19.95; and 40 dresses, each costing $8.75, and retailing at $15.95. Upon checking the shipment, she discovered that eight of the $19.95 dresses and six of the $15.95 dresses were colors and sizes that she had not ordered. She, therefore, returned them to the vendor.

   a. What was the total dollar amount at retail that she returned?
   b. What percentage of the shipment at retail was returned?

8. A salesperson, whose commissions average 15% of total sales, earned $72 in commissions during the week. What were the total sales he made during the week?

9. A store permitted a customer an allowance of $2.75 on a dress selling for $30. What was the percent of the allowance given the customer?

10. During a sale, a store advertised a raincoat for $59.95 with a reduction of 33⅓%.

   a. What was the dollar reduction offered?
   b. What was the new price of the raincoat?

NOTES

How to Use a Mini-Calculator

The proper use of a mini-calculator is vital to the successful results it can furnish. This helpful tool allows the user to combine speed with accuracy in most simple or more complex calculations.

For good results, practice the following Do's when using a mini-calculator:

1. Place mini-calculator on a firm surface in order to avoid the slipping of numbers and/or the mini-calculator.
2. Use the eraser end of a pencil to insert numbers to prevent marring the surfaces of the keys or to avoid striking more than one key.
3. Avoid dropping the mini-calculator.
4. As numbers are entered into the mini-calculator glance at the *screen* to insure that the desired digit(s) have been inserted.
5. If battery type of mini-calculator, become familiar with a fading battery which causes the numbers on the screen to lighten.

I. PROCEDURE FOR SIMPLE ARITHMETIC CALCULATION OF WHOLE NUMBERS

With whole numbers, the basic processes of addition, subtraction, multiplication and division can easily be completed through the use of the desired sign to calculate the particular process desired.

A. Addition Process

EXAMPLE: If you want to *add* 79 and 36, you would go through the following steps:
1. Press the ON Key.
2. Press the 7 key, and then the 9 key.
3. Press the addition (+) sign key.
4. Press the 3 key, and then the 6 key.
5. Press the equals (=) sign key, and presto your answer appears on the screen.

In the addition of numbers, it *would not* matter if you were to insert 79 *or* 36 first. 79 + 36 = 115 or 36 + 79 = 115.

B. Subtraction Process

In the subtraction process, essentially the same procedure for steps 1 and 2 is used, but for step 3, the *minus* sign is substituted before advancing to steps 4 and 5. In the subtraction process, the higher number(s) *must* be inserted first with the lower number(s) being entered *after* the minus sign.

EXAMPLE: If you want to *subtract* 36 from 79, you would:
1. Press the ON Key.
2. Press the 7 key, and then the 9 key.
3. Press the minus (−) sign key.
4. Press the 3 key, and then the 6 key.
5. Press the equals (=) sign key and the result 43 would appear.

C. Multiplication Process

In the multiplication of 79 × 36, the same procedure is used as in either the addition or subtraction process, except in step 3, the multiplication sign (×) is substituted. In this process, it does not matter whether you first insert 79 × 36 or 36 × 79, either one produces the answer of 2844.

D. Division Process

In the division of 79 by 36, or 79 ÷ 36, the *dividend* 79 *must* be entered first with the divisor 36 being inserted after the division sign.

EXAMPLE:
1. Insert 79.
2. Press the divide (÷) sign key.
3. Insert 36.
4. Press the equals (=) key and the quotient is 2.1944444.

Since division is merely a reverse process of multiplication, you can check the accuracy of your division by multiplying the quotient (2.1944444) by the divisor (36), which will give you the dividend of 78.999998 or 79.

II. PROCEDURE FOR SIMPLE ARITHMETIC CALCULATIONS OF WHOLE NUMBERS AND FRACTIONAL PARTS

When whole numbers and fractional parts are combined, the fractional parts should be expressed in decimals and the desired process of addition, subtraction, multiplication and/or division should be followed as explained.

EXAMPLE:
1. 2½ becomes 2.5 when inserted in the mini-calculator.
2. $5.49 is the value that is used when dealing with dollars and cents.

III. PROCEDURE FOR SIMPLE ARITHMETIC CALCULATIONS OF PERCENTAGES

Some mini-calculators have an arithmetic capability humans do not have. Test your own mini-calculator to see if it has the ability to multiply and/or subtract percentages without first converting the percent to a decimal and then converting the solution to a percent (%).

A. Multiplication Process

EXAMPLE: Multiply 500 × 25%.
The process can be as follows:
1. Insert 500.
2. Press the multiplication (×) key.
3. Insert 25.
4. Press the percent (%) key and the answer 125 appears on the screen.

An alternate process is:
1. Insert 500.
2. Press the multiplication (×) key.
3. Press the decimal (.) sign.
4. Insert 25.
5. Press the equals (=) sign and 125 appears.

B. Division Process

EXAMPLE: 500 ÷ 25%.
In the division of 500 ÷ 25%, the same procedure(s) can be followed:
1. Insert 500.
2. Press the division (÷) key.
3. Insert 25.
4. Press the percent (%) key, and the answer 2000 appears on the screen.

An alternate process is:
1. Insert 500.
2. Press the division (÷) key.
3. Insert the decimal (.) sign followed by 25.
4. Press the equals (=) sign and 2000 appears.

C. Subtraction of a % From a Whole Number

EXAMPLE: Subtract 25% from 500.
1. Insert 500.
2. Press the minus (−) sign.
3. Insert 25.
4. Press the percent (%) key and the answer 375 appears.

GLOSSARY

Allowance to Customer Partial refund or credit to compensate for merchandising deficiency such as missing buttons or parts; customer keeps merchandise.

Anticipation An extra fractional discount earned by retailers, under certain conditions, for payment of invoices prior to expiration of cash discount period.

Average Markup Composite of the relationship between all cost amounts and all retail amounts for a department or grouping of goods during a specified time period.

Average Stock The total of B.O.M. dollar inventory figures divided by the number of months considered.

Billed Cost The manufacturer's price for goods offered to a retailer.

B.O.M. Beginning of month.

Book Inventory Value, at retail price, of goods on hand at a given time. Also called *perpetual inventory*.

Cash Discount Percentage Deduction from cost of goods for conformance to prearranged terms of payment between vendor and retailer.

Charge Back Form on which the amounts of merchandise returned to resources by retailer for credit or refund is recorded.

Closeout A grouping of goods, usually composed of a broken assortment, offered by resource to retailer at a reduced cost price.

C.O.D. Cash on delivery.

Complement The difference between 100 and any number less than 100. (e.g., the complement of 60 is 40).

Cumulative Markup The total retail of all merchandise handled, season-to-date minus the invoiced cost of the merchandise before cash discounts are adjusted.

Customer Returns Dollar amount value of goods sent back to retailer by customer for credit or refund.

Dating An agreement specifying time period for payment of an invoice.

Department A grouping of related merchandise for which common records are kept.

Employee Discounts A percentage deducted from regular retail price as a courtesy to employees of a retail organization. Ranges from 10% to 30%.

EDP (Electronic Data Processing) The planned conversion of facts (as by computer) into usable or storable form to achieve a desired result.

E.O.M. End of month—usually designates dollar value of stock.

Expenses of Operation The overhead of doing business, e.g., salaries, rent, advertising, delivery, utilities.

Flash Report Daily report indicating sales amount.

F.O.B. Free-on-board. The way of expressing who is responsible for paying transportation charges.

F.O.B. Factory Retailer pays transportation.

F.O.B. Retailer Resource pays transportation.

Gross Margin   The remainder after subtracting total cost of goods from total retail amount of sales. Also called *gross profit*.

Gross Profit   See *Gross Margin*.

Gross Sales   Retail value of total initial sales prior to deduction of dollar amount returned by customers.

Initial Markup   The difference between the cost of goods and the original retail price; planned markup specified on orders for merchandise; a projected markup goal.

Inventory (*noun*)   Synonymous with the term "stock." See *Stock*.

Inventory (*verb*)   To actively count and record quantities of merchandise for the purpose of determining a total dollar value of goods on hand.

Invoice   A bill presented by a vendor to a retailer for goods purchased.

Inward Transportation   Cost of carrying goods from resource to retailer, e.g., trucking, freight, postage.

Journal or Purchase Record   Consolidated listing of invoice amounts, transportation charges, discounts.

List Price   A retail level price generally set by manufacturers.

Maintained Markup   The difference between the cost of goods and the actual selling price.

Markdown   A reduction in retail price, generally for the purpose of moving slow selling goods out more rapidly.

Markup   A percentage, based on retail price, which generates the needed dollar difference between cost and retail price.

Merchandise Loans   Goods given temporarily to another department or division for purposes other than resale, such as display.

Merchandise Plan   A "roadmap," usually set up twice annually, indicating planned sales, markdowns, stocks, and purchases.

Merchandise Transfers   Goods "bought or sold" internally, from one department to another, for purposes of resale to ultimate customer.

Net Period   Span of time between expiration of eligibility for cash discount and start of penalty period.

Net Sales   Gross sales minus reductions.

Open-to-buy (OTB)   The amount of unspent money available for purchasing merchandise during a given period.

Overage   Dollar difference between book stock figure and physical count figure when the *latter* is the larger of the two.

Perpetual Inventory   See *Book Inventory*.

Physical Inventory   The retail dollar value of all goods physically present in a periodic stock count.

P.O.S. Point-of-sale.

Prepaid Payment of transportation charges by vendor when merchandise is shipped.

Price Change Form Form on which markdowns, additional markup and cancellation or markdown are tallied.

Price Line A predetermined retail level figure which is aimed at a specific market segment.

Profit on Sales The dollar amount remaining after costs and expenses are paid.

Quantity Discount A percentage deduction from billed cost allowable when the dollar amount or unit quantity on an order for goods (or a cumulative figure for a period of time) falls within certain predesignated limits.

Reductions from Retail Diminution of retail value of sales due to markdowns, employee discounts, shrinkage.

Remittance Payment.

Retail The marketing level at which goods are sold to the ultimate customer.

Retail Merchandising The science of offering goods to ultimate customers at the right price, the right form, at the right location, and at an appropriate time.

Retail Price The price at which an ultimate customer purchases goods from a store or other retail firm.

R.O.G. Receipt of goods.

Season Letter A code letter indicating date of item's entry into stock.

Shortage Dollar difference between book stock figure and physical count figures when the *former* is the larger of the two.

Shrinkage Lessening of retail value of stock on hand, generally due to theft or breakage.

Stock Goods on hand at a given time expressed as a dollar amount.

Stock-Sales Ratio The proportion between the B.O.M. stock figure and the dollar amount of planned sales for the same month.

Terms of Sale Arrangement between merchandise source and retailer relative to time period for payment of invoice.

Total Cost of Goods Billed cost *plus* workroom charges *minus* cash discount.

Trade Discount A percentage or series of percentages deducted from list price, thereby determining cost price.

Turnover The number of times at which the average investment in merchandise (at retail value) is bought and sold in a given period.

Vendor A merchandise resource such as a manufacturer, jobber, distributor.

Volume The retail value of sales for a given period, usually expressed annually.

Workroom Charges Amounts attributed to alteration and preparation of goods.

REFERENCE READINGS

Bellenger, Danny N. & Jac L. Goldstucker. *Retailing Basics.* Homewood, Illinois: Richard D. Irwin, Inc., 1983.

Bohlinger, Maryanne Smith. *Merchandise Buying: A Practical Guide,* Second Edition. Englewood Cliffs, New Jersey: Prentice-Hall, Inc., 1983.

Morgenstein, Melvin & Harriet Strongin. *Modern Retailing: Principles and Practices.* New York: John Wiley & Sons, 1983.

Ostrow, Rona & Sweetman R. Smith. *The Dictionary of Retailing.* New York: Fairchild Publications, 1985.

Packard, Sidney, Arthur A. Winters & Nathan Axelrod. *Fashion Buying and Merchandising.* New York: Fairchild Publications, 1983.

Stone, Elaine. *Fashion Buying,* First Edition. New York: McGraw-Hill, 1987.

Wingate, John W. & Joseph Friedlander. *The Management of Retail Buying,* Second Edition. Englewood Cliffs, New Jersey: Prentice-Hall, Inc., 1978.